Plate I.   *Frontispiece.*

PORTION OF LINEN COLLAR.

With border and broad ends of rose point.   Venetian, seventeenth century.

OLD LACE
A Handbook for Collectors

AN ACCOUNT OF THE DIFFERENT
STYLES OF LACE · THEIR HISTORY,
CHARACTERISTICS & MANUFACTURE

BY

M. JOURDAIN

JOINT-EDITOR OF PALLISER'S " HISTORY OF LACE "

WITH 163 EXAMPLES ON NINETY-
FIVE PLATES FROM PHOTOGRAPHS

B. T. BATSFORD LTD · LONDON

First published 1908
This edition first published 1988
© B. T. Batsford Ltd 1988

ISBN 0 7134 5077 0

Printed in Great Britain by
Butler & Tanner Ltd
Frome, Somerset
for the Publishers
B. T. Batsford Ltd
4 Fitzhardinge Street
London W1H 0AH

PREFACE.

IT may, perhaps, seem necessary to give some reason for the appearance of a new work dealing with hand-made lace, especially as two books on this subject have appeared in England alone in the course of the year. It has been suggested to me, however, by many collectors, that the *historical* aspect of lace has been dealt with in previous works, almost to the exclusion of its technical and artistic side. Mrs Palliser's history (first issued in 1865), which I re-edited in 1902, is almost exhaustive in certain aspects, and a storehouse of valuable material collected by the author relative not only to the history of lace, but of embroidery and costume. But even since 1902 new material, new facts have come to light in works dealing with lace of various countries.

I have, therefore, in this book, while giving the chief landmarks in the history of each lace in each important centre of production —especially those that affected the quality and design of the lace produced—included or referred to these fresh facts and information. The French have been especially diligent in investigating the origins and development of their national industries. I have also been interested in tracing, where possible, the influence of contemporary art and design upon the development of lace, which is, naturally, largely subject to the influences of and fashions in textiles, as may be seen by a comparison of French patterned textiles with laces of the three great periods which correspond roughly to the reigns of Louis XIV., XV., and XVI.

As the very large number of illustrations in each chapter are arranged in order of date, it will be easy for readers to follow this progress. For this reason, dated pieces—though these are naturally rare—have been illustrated wherever possible.

Another very interesting subject which has not hitherto been fully treated is the influence of lace of one country upon the lace of another, *i.e.,* that of Italian lace upon Points de France, of French design upon Mechlin of the Louis XV. period, &c.

The comparison and dating of laces have been rendered much more possible since the period when Mrs Palliser wrote, by the improvement in public museums at home and abroad, which have in many cases published portfolios of their lace collections.

Some account of the differences in manufacture of real and machine-made lace, and enlarged illustrations showing their essential differences in texture, will, I hope, be of use to collectors.

Many of these chapters appeared originally in the *Connoisseur*, but have since been revised ; and I have to thank the courtesy of the editor for the loan of some of the blocks.

M. JOURDAIN.

Broadwinsor, Dorset.
November 1908.

CONTENTS

b

OLD LACE.

CHAPTER I.—INTRODUCTION.

THE DATE OF THE ORIGIN OF LACE-MAKING—TESTS FOR REAL LACE.

" LACE is the name applied to an ornamental open-work of threads of flax, cotton, silk, gold, or silver, and occasionally of mohair or aloe fibre. Such threads may be either looped, or plaited, or twisted together in one of three ways : (1) with a needle, when the work is distinctively known as 'needlepoint lace'; (2) with bobbins, pins on a pillow or cushion, when the work is known as 'pillow lace'; * (3) by machinery." †

It is the two former processes, *i.e.*, hand-made lace, that we have to consider.

The origin of hand-made lace is obscure. Flanders and Italy both claim its invention, but there is distinct evidence that Flemish lace was later than the Italian, in the fact that Flanders published no lace pattern-book until that of Jean de Glen at Liège, in 1597, and de Glen in his preface himself says that he brought his patterns from Italy. They are a transcript from Vinciolo. A pattern-book published

---

* Or "bobbin lace," which is the more convenient term, as needlepoint lace is also made upon a pillow.

† Art. *Lace*, Encyclopædia Britannica.

A

by "R. M." about the year 1550* at Zürich, by Christoff Froschower,† gives proof that bobbin lace was known in Venice before 1526.

It says that "the art of lace-making ('die kuenst der Dentel-schnuren') has been known and practised for about twenty-five years in our country, for it was first brought by merchants from Venice and Italy into Germany in the year 1526. . . . Clever women and girls admiring it, continued with great industry and zeal to copy and re-produce the same . . . and invented new models much more beauti-ful than the first." ‡

At the end of the sixteenth century bobbin and needlepoint lace was made in Flanders, as well as in Italy, and pattern-books were issued having the same general character as those published in Italy. France and England followed Italy and Flanders in adopting lace, and towards the close of the seventeenth century a great State-subsidised enterprise, the establishment of a lace industry, took place in France under the advice of Colbert, the minister of Louis XIV. In these French centres Italian needlepoint was chiefly copied. The lace made in Germany,§ Sweden, Russia, Spain, Denmark, Switzerland, and Austria, did not result in work of any high artistic quality or importance, and is not treated in this book.

In Belgium (though Brussels acquired some celebrity for her needle-made laces), very fine and artistic bobbin lace was produced ; and

---

* This date is given as 1536 in Mrs Bury Palliser's " History of Lace," and in E. Lefébure's " Broderie et Dentelles."

† Printed verbatim in Ilgs' " Geschichte und Terminologie der alten Spitzen," p. 31.

‡ The author continues: " In my opinion the art has now reached its highest point." Women " could earn a better living at lace than with spindle, needle, shuttle, or anything else of the kind." " At first these laces were only used for sheets, but now they have come to be used on collarettes, round the necks of bodices, on sleeves, caps, as edgings and bindings, on and round aprons and barber's cloths (or coarse cloths), on handkerchiefs, table and other linen, pillows and bedclothes, besides many other things which I need not mention." The author suggests varying the laces by the use of coloured threads. The patterns resemble the more elementary and least successful patterns of " Le Pompe " for plaited lace. Quoted in " Pillow Lace : a Practical Handbook," E. Minkoff.

§ A certain Barbara Uttmann of Nuremberg instructed the peasants of the Hartz Mountains in lace-making in 1561.

like Belgium, Flanders produced almost exclusively bobbin laces. From Flemish laces is derived the English Honiton.

The collector of old lace, unlike the collector of old silver, prints, china, enamels, and the like, has not to fear delicate and almost omnipresent fraud. A box of modern enamel may be produced by methods similar to those by which an old Battersea enamel box was produced, and when painted by a clever French workman (who copies an original piece) and finally chipped by the dealer, it would, and does, deceive the very elect. The new box is in the process of its manufacture, and in all essentials, like the old. This, however, is not the case with imitations of either embroidery or lace. The methods of production of real and of machine-made lace differ essentially. There is no deceptive quality in imitation lace, which is practically never described or sold as real lace in the shop of any lace-dealer.

Needlepoint lace, in which a single needle and thread are alone used to form the pattern, which is built up entirely of button-hole stitch and other loopings, has never been successfully imitated by the machine, which cannot produce a button-hole stitch.

Bobbin lace is more closely imitated than needlepoint by machine, but even here the texture is not to be mistaken for that of bobbin lace. The machine does not attempt to make a regular plait.*

The man who most materially aided in the development of the lace machine was John Heathcoat, who was born in 1783. His interest in the making of lace had been aroused by seeing a skilled bobbin lacemaker at work. He began his experiments by patiently drawing out threads from hand-made lace, and attentively watching the direction they followed. He found that the majority of them were dealt with in a regular fashion, some going lengthwise and scarcely varying their direction, the others travelling backwards and forwards across the width. This led him to construct a machine in which half the threads were on a beam, while the twisting was done by the remaining threads, carried in to those which passed between the longitudinal beam threads. Since Heathcoat's day the details of construction rather than essential principles have been improved. " The bobbins of the weft

---

* A French machine, " La Dentellière " (see *La Nature*, 3rd March 1881), produced plaited work, but the expense of this was as great as that of pillow lace, and it has never been adopted.

threads as they pass like pendulums between the warp threads are made to oscillate, and through this oscillation the threads twist themselves or become twisted with the warp threads."* As the twistings take place, combs passing through both warp and weft threads compress the twistings. Thus the usual machine-made lace may generally be detected by its compressed twisted threads.

This consequent ribbed appearance of the toilé is present in machine-made imitations of every kind of pillow lace, and serves most easily to detect it when compared with the flat and even appearance of the toilé of hand-made lace (see Plate II.). In the real lace also the meshes are slightly irregular.

Of bobbin laces the most successfully rendered in machine lace are Valenciennes and Mechlin, but there is a clumsiness in the rendering of detail, and the poor readily torn edge of the machine-made lace is noticeable when compared with the hand-made. Mechlin is remarkable for its cordonnet of thick flat thread outlining the ornament. The first imitation Mechlin left out this distinctive feature, and at the International Exhibition of 1867 Nottingham exhibited imitation Mechlin, in which the cordonnet was run on by hand. At present modern imitation Mechlin is provided with the cordonnet of stout cotton which is often cut at certain points in the design (as the design in Mechlin is not continuous). The cut ends are not firmly fastened down, and break away readily, especially after washing.

The finer qualities of Brussels, remarkable for the fidelity and grace with which floral compositions are rendered, it is impossible to reproduce in the relatively coarse machine-made cotton.

In addition to these special differences, Séguin in his book " La Dentelle" gives a general reason why machine-made lace cannot equal the handwork it imitates: " In machine work the operating force is uniform, continually the same, hence there is always an equal tension in the threads and a perfectly regular tissue is produced, but at the same time perfectly flat. Handwork, on the contrary, is bound to be irregular because, though the worker's hand represents a force of uniform strength, its action is unequal and cannot be regulated in the same way as can a mechanical force." He proceeds to show the

* Art. *Lace*, Encyclopædia Britannica.

Plate II.

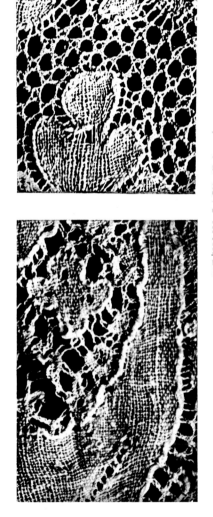

MECHLIN LACE (Enlarged).

IMITATION MECHLIN (Enlarged).

advantage of this regularity by alluding to the uneven surface of hand-woven cashmere shawls, which " present an infinite succession of waves and little imperceptible roughnesses which catch the light and cast shadows," making a surface vastly different from anything a machine can produce, " different in somewhat the same way in which the inside of a limpet shell differs from that of a ' sea-ear.' The one is flat, dead white, the other by its irregularities breaks the light into prismatic colours we call mother-of-pearl, and these colours depend only on the uneven surface of the shell ; a cast taken in sealing-wax will reproduce them."

The best flax thread is too soft to bear the tension needed by a machine, hence the poor " cottony " texture of machine laces.

The variability of texture is easily recognised by people who are accustomed to look for the small but significant marks of the tool or the hand in works of art. This irregularity can be seen more readily under a lens.

The making up of flowers from Italian rose point is the only " faking " which is possible in lace, and this is really only the re-arrangement of genuine old pieces.

In rose point the brides are more liable to be destroyed than the relatively thick and solid ornament ; lace-menders replace the brides, and this is a legitimate branch of lace-mending. In some specimens, however, it is easy to avoid replacing the brides, by forcing the details of the ornament to touch one another. An exceptional piece now and then appears to have been made without brides, like the collar of rose point in the Musée de Cluny (Plate XXIV.), or with a minimum of brides, as in a fine specimen in the Victoria and Albert Museum (see frontispiece), but for the most part specimens without brides should be looked upon with suspicion.

In pieces that have been forcibly dealt with, the scroll design, originally free, and linked by its background of brides, is wrenched and bent from a natural to a debased, flattened, or irregular curve in order that portions of the design may touch one another. Such specimens can be recognised by the overlapping and encroachment of certain details, and by the absence of continuity of design. As it is often impossible to fill up the required space with the scroll in its new position, detached flowers with no relation to the original design are sewn in, the main line of the scroll is broken again and again, and the whole piece presents a fortuitous concourse of ornamental detail.

In clumsily pieced specimens (such as Plate XXVI.), one flower can be seen overlapping part of the ornament; a small detached flower is often suspended in an open space without any connection with a stalk or scroll. The scroll in its new position often wrinkles, and will not lie flat. As the flowers are often taken from pieces of different design and quality, the difficulty of combining them into a continuous or even coherent pattern can readily be imagined, and certain portions appear thicker and heavier than others. In more carefully treated specimens, the thickness and heaviness of the bride-less design alone is visible.

CHAPTER II.

LACIS OR DARNED NETTING.

DRAWN-THREAD work was known in Egypt in the earliest times, and examples of this work are to be seen in the mummy cloths in the Egyptian room of the British Museum. The withdrawal of threads from linen is the simplest form of its ornamentation of linen. The material in old Italian drawn-work is usually loosely woven ; certain threads were drawn out from the ground and others left, upon and between which needlework was made. The withdrawal of threads regulated the pattern to be produced ; a curved scroll or a circle had to be approximately rendered in small squares. The background of such work appeared to consist of a net of square meshes.

What is known as *Lacis* is darned work upon a network of meshes (known as *réseau*, *rézel*, *rézeuil*), which we learn from the pattern-book of Matthias Mignerak (1605) was made by beginning a single stitch and increasing a stitch on each side until the required size was obtained, then the square was finished by reducing a stitch upon each side until it was reduced to one.

Lacis, though generally a term applied to the réseau when embroidered, was also occasionally used for the réseau itself. Such is its use in the " Béle Prérie contenant divers caracters, et differentes sortes de lettres alphabetiques . . . pour appliquer sur le reseuil ou iassis" (Paris, 1601), and in the lines of Skelton quoted on next page. Mary, Queen of Scots, referred to her lacis-work as "ouvres masches" (Fr., *mailles ;* Ital., *maglia**). Cotgrave† gives, among other meanings of *maille*, "a mash of a net, the square hole that is between thread and thread."

The *réseuil* was generally of linen thread, sometimes of silk or gold. Lacis were sometimes made in a long border or panel, at other times in small squares, which, joined together and combined with cutwork, were much used for bed hangings, table-cloths, &c. Prominent parts of the design were sometimes thrown into relief by

---

* " *Maglia* is properly the holes in any net. Also a shirt or jacket of mail" (Florio, "A Worlde of Wordes").

† Randle Cotgrave, " Dictionarie of the French and English Tongues," 1611.

a thicker outlining thread—the forerunner of the cordonnet in lace. The darning is sometimes quite even in workmanship, at other times it is of different degrees of strength, lighter for certain portions of the surface, and heavier for others, thus producing a shaded effect. Relief is very seldom obtained; but in a fine piece with a vine pattern in the Victoria and Albert Museum, the grapes are raised into a considerable degree of convexity by tightly sewing round each portion of the canvas ground which had been previously darned so as to represent a grape.

A book containing designs for lacis was issued at Cologne, by P. Quentell. The patterns consist of borders, alphabets, &c., some on white, others on black, ground; some with counted stitches. The earliest edition extant is dated 1527; Quentell, however, refers to a previous edition, hence M. Séguin obviously puts the date of its invention too late when he gives 1520 as the approximate limit of its earliest use. In a painting by Lorenzo Costa in S. Giacomo, at Bologna (1488), the square openings of the dresses of the three persons depicted are filled in with a border of lacis. Knotted net (probably ornamented) was very much used in church work for lectern and frontal veils, and pyx cloths and "corporals," as early as the fourteenth century, and Rock in his "Textile Fabrics" quotes from Dugdale's "St Paul's": "St Paul's, London, had a cushion covered with knotted thread" ("pulvinar copertum de albo filo nodato"). Network (filatorium) was probably another name for this darned net; in the "Exeter Inventory" we read that its cathedral possessed, A.D. 1327, three pieces of it for use at the altar, and one for throwing over the desk ("tria filatoria linea, unde unum pro desco").

The earliest mention of lacis, by name, is to be found in the lines of the "laureate" Skelton (1460-1529), which also contain the earliest literary reference to samplers:

> "When that the tapettes and carpettes were layd
> Whereon theis ladys softly myght rest,
> The saumpler to sew on, the lacis to embraid."

Another argument against dating lacis only from the first quarter of the sixteenth century is the exceedingly archaic character of the design of some specimens; the work also must have been widely known before it created the demand for a pattern-book. The patterns for lacis which form the greater part of the designs of the early Italian and German pattern-books * until Vinciolo could be also used for embroidery in short and cross stitches. The earliest designs are conventional diapers. Subject designs and religious emblems, however, were soon introduced, and Vavassore gives patterns of a large flower-pot, mermaid, Paschal lamb, and a double plate representing Orpheus playing to the beasts. "Marriage groups, the bridegroom with a flower, the bride with a fan, and behind, a procession of tiny cavaliers and ladies; hunting scenes, animals of every species; rows of mermaids, winged lions, and cocks, dogs, stags, and eagles, forming a border to the central ornament. Castles, towers, falconers —"whole scenes to which we have now lost the key," are to be found among the designs for lacis.† The most influential designer, both for lacis and cutwork, was Vinciolo, the first edition of whose work‡ was published in 1587. The second half of this edition contains designs representing the seven planets—Sol, Luna, Mars, Mercury, Jupiter, Venus, and Saturn. Four in squares of various designs, two of Amorini shooting stags and birds; Neptune and the winds, an arabesque with impresa of a column with circle and double triangle; five borders and squares, and "two bordures à carreaux." The interest of Vinciolo's work is that specimens of lacis are extant which reproduce his designs. In the Victoria and Albert Museum there is a specimen of lacis§ representing designs similar to those of Vinciolo. This bed-cover is composed of a series of squares, darned with representations of the months of the year, male and female heads, figures and groups. There is also a piece in the Musée de Cluny very much in Vinciolo's style.

In the second part of the edition of 1588, in his "Advertisement au

---

* The earliest known pattern-book now appears to be that of Jorg Gastel of Zwickau, 1525, a copy of which has recently been added to the collection in the Königliche Kunstgewerbe Bibliothek, Dresden. Next in order of date seems to come the publication of P. Quentell of Cologne, "Eyn new Kuntslich boich," 1527. In the same year and at the same town appeared "Liure noveau et subtil touchant l'art et sciéce" of "matrepiere Quinty." See "Early Pattern-books of Lace, Embroidery, and Needlework," by Edward F. Strange (*Transactions of the Bibliographical Society*, vol. vii.).

† Elise Ricci, "Antiche trine Italiane."

‡ "Les Singuliers et Nouveaux Pourtraicts et Ouvrages de Lingerie," Paris, 1587.

§ No. 109, acquired in 1884.

Lecteur," Vinciolo says that having promised, since the first impression of his book, to give a "nouvelle bande d'ouvrages," and not to disappoint certain ladies who have complained that he has not made "du reseau assez beau à leur fantaisie," he wished for the third time to place before their eyes many new and different patterns of "reseau de point conté que j'ay cousus et attachez à la fin de mes premières figures." After the thirty plates already published, follow the twenty additional of "reseau de point conté," consisting of the lion, pelican, unicorn, stag, peacock, griffon, and the four seasons, &c. Lacis was frequently combined with point coupé or reticella in the late sixteenth and seventeenth centuries, when the combination was known as punto reale a reticella. Elisabetta Catenea Parasole (1616) gives designs for this type of work, which made use of small squares of lacis.

In a pattern-book * in the National Art Library is one for lacis, bearing the name of Elizabeth, the eldest daughter of Frederick II., King of Denmark and Norway, and Sophia of Mecklenburg, who was the second wife of Henry Julius, Duke of Brunswick-Wolfenbuttel, Calenburg, and Blankenburg (1589-1613), and is dated two years after the death of the latter. It contains the arms of Denmark, a quaint representation of the Child Jesus, Jacob wrestling with an angel, the two spies with the bunch of grapes, Samson and the lion, Satan being chained by the angel, the four evangelists, &c.; also emblems of faith, hope, charity, justice, prudence, the story of the prodigal son, and a (double-page) dance of Saxon peasants.

In comparing characteristic specimens of German and Italian lacis and German and Italian pattern-books, we see that in the German designs eagles and heraldic emblems, oak leaves, acorns, thistles, and hunting scenes are often met with; in the Italian lacis the foliage is more conventional in character. Some squares of German lacis in the Kunstgewerbe Museum at Leipzig show coats of arms darned in a variety of stitches, with a raised cordonnet forming the outline. Some of the designs in this Museum are conventional, in others

---

* The book is a MS., the draughtsman is unknown, and there are no indications of place of origin beyond the association with the person whose name it bears. There is no title-page, but the first leaf bears the arms of Denmark. It was described and illustrated in the *Magazine of Art*, vol. xxvi., pp. 179, 180, by Edward F. Strange.

Plate III.

PART OF A BAND OF LACIS.

Italian, late sixteenth century.

OBLONG PIECE OF LACIS.

Patterns of birds and beasts among trees. A representation of the Creation. Italian, sixteenth century.

an attempt at naturalistic effects appears. Pieces of German make are frequently of a loosely made net, and of coarse linen thread. Germany, however, in the sixteenth and seventeenth centuries was renowned for its lacis and embroidery with thread on net, of which there are several good examples in the Victoria and Albert Museum. But it is exceedingly difficult to assign a specimen of lacis to any definite country, there is but little refinement in the manner of working, and often little differentiation in design. The finer qualities were, no doubt, made in Italy. A very coarse type was made in Spain, of interest from the bold and naïf designs. Much lacis was produced in France under Catherine de Médicis, the patroness of Vinciolo, and the popularity of the work is proved by the number of editions of Vinciolo's work printed in Paris from 1587 to 1623, and by the fact that his designs were copied.*

Italian lacis shows richer and more conventional designs than those of any other country. An angular scroll with a conventional vine-leaf is frequently met with (Plate III.), and curious Renaissance fantasies, tritons, terminal figures, or figures with foliated extremities, such as are met with in the decoration of the period, are combined with effective scroll designs. In Southern Italy and Sicily the influence of Oriental taste was of necessity more direct than in the north. In other South Italian and Sicilian lacis small skirted figures, holding up their hand, and other traditional motifs, are represented.

Cretan lacis is especially interesting, from the combination of the Italian structure of ornament and the strange way in which that system, with its cultured knowledge of form and balance, has been misinterpreted by the Cretan workers. There is a certain quaint almost grotesque air common to all the specimens of Cretan lacis, and it is especially pronounced in the human, quadruped, and bird figures which are introduced into the midst of the conventional branchage and foliage. The pink is a prominent feature in the design as in Cretan embroidery. The lacis is frequently divided into three portions—the most important central piece, and two narrow borders or insertions at top and bottom.

* The title of Jean de Glen's pattern-book, "Les singuliers et nouveaux pourtraits, pour toutes sortes de lingeries," published at Liège in 1597, is borrowed from Vinciolo, and the plates are mostly drawn from his.

CHAPTER III.

CUTWORK (RETICELLA) AND PUNTO IN ARIA.

LACE appears to be of Italian origin, though attempts have been made to trace it to Oriental sources. Though, however, it is impossible to prove that the work of the earliest laces was borrowed by Italy from the East, or from the Saracens of Sicily,* or from the Greeks who took refuge in Italy from the troubles of the Lower Empire,† the influence of Oriental design upon the early geometric laces is a hitherto unrecognised fact. Venice in Italy was peculiarly fitted by her position to transmit Oriental influences. There are documents that prove that in 1390 the Venetians traded with India and had a consul at Siam. Venice was the great emporium and distributor of metal-work, silk, cloth of gold, which came to her from Constantinople and Greece; and in the fifteenth century Venetian commerce covered the whole of the civilised world. In furniture, the *intarsia* or inlaid work, which was in such favour in the sixteenth century, shows in its design the obvious influence of Eastern art; and in many cases the patterns have been taken directly from Arab sources. The same influence shows itself in the stuffs, embroideries, damascened metal-work, and other such objects, of which the industries were naturally directly affected by the importation of Eastern models and Eastern methods. The influence of the East upon European ceramic art and the artistic pottery of the fourteenth and fifteenth centuries, espe-

---

* Francesco Nardi, "Sull' Origine dell' Arte del Ricamo," Padova, 1839: "What further confirms its Byzantine origin is that those very places which kept up the closest intercourse with the Greek Empire are the cities where point lace was earliest made and flourished to the greatest extent," *e.g.*, Venice.

† Digby Wyatt, "Industrial Arts of the Nineteenth Century."

Plate IV.

Ouurages de point coupé

A DESIGN FOR CUTWORK (Reticella).
From Vinciolo, "Les Singuliers et Nouveaux Pourtraicts," 1587.

Plate V.

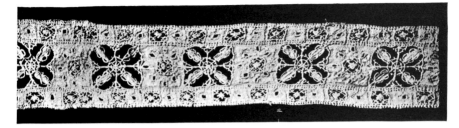

STRIP OF LINEN.
With squares filled in with cutwork (Reticella).

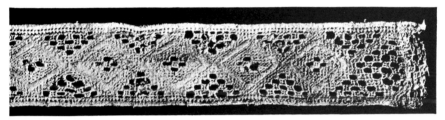

CUTWORK (Reticella).

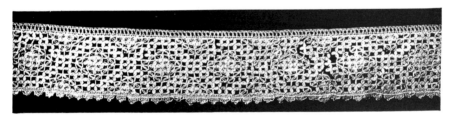

CUTWORK (Reticella).
The lines of the linen foundation entirely covered with needlepoint.

VANDYKED EDGING OF NEEDLEPOINT.

Plate VI.

PATTERNS FOR EDGINGS AND INSERTIONS OF NEEDLEPOINT.
From Cesare Vecellio, "Corona delle Nobili et Virtuose Donne," 1592.

EDGING OF NEEDLEPOINT LACE.

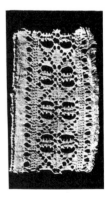

PIECE OF DRAWN WORK.

cially that of Italy, has been noticed. "In the painting of the Coronation of the Virgin, by a pupil or follower of Giotto, in the National Gallery, there is a band of ornament on the upright of the step beneath the throne, composed of stars and crosses, as in Persian wall-tiles. Again, in the picture of the Circumcision, by Marco Marziale, in this Gallery, star shapes, similar to the tiles, figure in the ornamentation of a linen cloth." * As Venice † was the place where embroidery and trimming of white linen first came into fashion in Europe, the motives of Oriental design—these same stars and crosses —were first applied to linen ornamentation in Venice, and it is possible that from Persian drawn-thread work with whipped stitches— possibly of the late fifteenth or early sixteenth century—the Italian art of drawing out threads and stitching over them was derived.‡

What were these principles of design thus borrowed? § Interlaced, repeating star-shaped and polygonal ornament, purely geometrical ; never naturalistic, or combined with figured ornament.

These geometrical forms are exclusively used in early Italian reticella and *punto in aria*, at a date when flowing scrolls and conventionalised flower ornament was freely used in the designs for embroidery.‖

The successive types of lace we have to consider are : cutwork, or reticella ; and its derivative *punto in aria*.

Cutwork is a term which is also used for reticella or Greek lace, which is its trade name. Reticella, first mentioned in the Sforza Inventory (1493), is not named in the pattern-books until Vecellio (1592). It is worked upon linen as a foundation ; threads were

---

* Henry Wallis, "The Godman Collection of Persian Ceramic Art belonging to F. Du Cane Godman, with examples from other Collections," London, 1894.

† Venetian linens for fine towelling and napery in general at one time were in favourite use during the fifteenth century. In the "Ducs de Bourgogne," by the Comte de Laborde, more than once we meet with such an entry as : "Une pièce de nappes, ouvraige de Venise," &c.

‡ A. S. Cole, *Journal of the Society of Arts*, 26th July 1895.

§ "On peut considérer l'art arabe comme étant un système de décoration fondé tout entier sur l'ordre et la forme géométriques, et qui n'emprunte rien ou presque rien à l'observation de la nature" (J. Bourgoin, "Les Arts Arabes," 1873).

‖ "L'idée qui domine dans le dessin des premières dentelles ne se rattache, par aucun côté, aux tendances de l'art décoratif du siècle où elles furent créées" (J. Séguin, "La Dentelle").

withdrawn or cut out of the linen to form the open spaces, and the remaining threads overcast with button-hole stitches (see Plate XI.). The effect of this work is identical with that of the geometric patterned needlepoint lace (early *punto in aria*); and the same patterns are equally suited to both classes of drawn linen and needlepoint lace, as may be seen by an examination of Vinciolo's pattern-book. The drawing out of the threads, by means of which the framework necessary for the reticella pattern was produced, was more laborious than the construction of skeleton frameworks of thread, firmly tacked down upon a piece of parchment—the foundation of *punto in aria*.* The crossings of these intersecting lines of thread were secured, and then all the foundation threads were covered with the button-hole stitch. The elaboration of this foundation into solid pattern was effected by adding row upon row of button-hole stitches, sometimes close, sometimes open in effect. These skeleton designs were made in squares, and by joining several similar bits together a long border was constructed. Some reticella made in Sicily and Southern Italy is embroidered rather heavily upon the solid portions of the ornament.

The basis of design in both types of lace is very similar. According to the pattern-books it is open squares or diamond shapes with diagonals from corner to corner, and two bars from side to side, the diagonals and bars crossing one another at the common centre, and so forming a radiation of eight lines bounded by a square. In the earliest examples the geometrical forms are simple; the details of the ornament touch one another. Later, the design becomes more refined and complicated, and picots or small loops are freely used. In some late specimens of *punto in aria* of the seventeenth century there is a raised rib upon the design, and some have the pattern emphasised by a raised button-hole stitched border. The restriction of design to a series or combination of squares (the constructive basis of reticella), is broken through in later specimens, and curved lines are introduced; the next step was the fuller mastery of design, shown in the representation of figures of light scroll designs. This change in the character of *punto in aria* took place at the very close of the sixteenth century,

---

* The term is first mentioned in Taglienti, "Opera nuova che insegna a le Dōne a cuscire. . . ." Venice, 1530. Brunet gives an edition dated 1528. In Taglienti it is mentioned as a stitch in embroidery.

Plate VII.

DETAIL IN A FRESCO.

In the Palazzo Pubblico at Siena.   By Ambrogio Lorenzetti.
(See openwork ornamentation on cushion.)

Plate VIII.

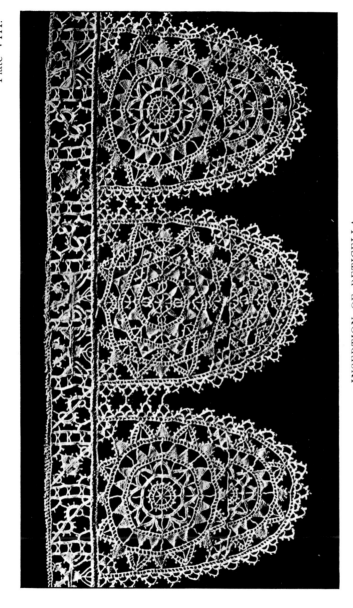

INSERTION OF RETICELLA.

With deep scallops of needlepoint. Late sixteenth or seventeenth century.

Plate IX.

NEEDLEPOINT BORDER.

Venetian, sixteenth or seventeenth century.

when the pattern-books give all varieties of odd figures to be worked
on lace.* One design of Vecellio represents, within a border with a
dentated edge, a harp, guitar, fiddle, horn, organ, trumpets, and pipes ;
and dolphins, running hounds, hunting scenes, Amorini, and mythological figures, are commonly introduced. In the collection of Mrs
John Hungerford Pollen is a chalice cover representing the figure of
St Peter with Bible and keys, supported by cherubs. Greek and
Levantine work of the seventeenth century introduce curious archaic
figures and devices with vases and stiff flower sprays.

In spite of the development of *punto in aria* reticella was in Italy
not entirely abandoned even as late as the nineteenth century. In
1862 a certain Francesco Bulgarini was still living at Siena who made
reticella of extreme fineness.†

In pictures I have found very little lace until the second quarter
of the sixteenth century. ‡ White lace has been *said* to be found in a
portrait of a lady, by Carpaccio (1476-1522), in the gallery at Venice,§
but I have not been able to trace this picture. In other pictures by
Carpaccio there is no lace and but little embroidery, and the linen is
for the most part plain; in one case embroidery in cross-stitch appears.
No lace is to be found in the paintings of Mantegna (1431-1506) or of
Luini ‖ (1470-1530). In the work of Pinturicchio (1454-1513) embroidery of cord or metal gimp is applied in conventional patterns to
the borders of dresses.¶ To judge by Italian painting, there is no

---

* In Parasole (1616) the patterns for "*ponti* in aria" are varied, apparently to
show variety in stitch, some of which are close, some open. The *punti* in aria
patterns are most rich and varied, and include in almost every design grotesque
figures and animals.

† Elise Ricci, "Antiche trine Italiane."

‡ Cav. A. Merli cites as the earliest known painting in which lace occurs, a
majolica disc, after the style of the Della Robbia family, in which is represented
the half figure of a lady, dressed in rich brocade, with a collar of white lace. As
the precise date cannot be fixed, and the work may be by one of Luca Della
Robbia's descendants, this, as evidence, is useless.

§ "The cuffs of the lady are edged with a narrow lace, the pattern of which
appears in Vecellio's 'Corona,' not published till 1591" (Lefébure).

‖ In Luini's "Presentation in the Temple" geometric cutwork or embroidery
appears on the priest's robe.

¶ Later, lace appears more frequently. In Titian (1477-1576) narrow lace is
used to edge shirts and shirt sleeves in female costumes. In the Prado Museum,

evidence of Cav. A. Merli's theory that " the art was even at the apex of perfection at the commencement of 1500"!

An exceptionally early instance of what appears to be needlepoint fillings of open spaces in a linen cushion is to be seen in a fresco by Ambrogio Lorenzetti (completed in 1339) in the Public Palace of Siena (Plate VII.). Here Pax reclines upon a linen cushion with an openwork seam and diamond-shaped openings filled in with star-like devices. Simple work of this nature, approximating to embroidery, was no doubt produced as early as fine linen was in use in Venice.

Of the pattern-books, the earliest in date we know of is 1525.* There may, however, have been earlier lost editions. Vavassore † begins the first book of his we know of by saying, " Havedo io pel passato alcuni libri di esempli" (" having made myself in the past some books of patterns"). The patterns are described as being for *recami*.

In that by Alessandro Pagannino, dated Venice, 1527—putting aside the author's ascription to himself of the credit of having published the first book on the subject—neither patterns nor titles indicate lace work. The first six cuts are designs for embroidery, the rest designs upon squares to be used for lacis or embroidery. In the work by Antonio Taglienti, 1530,‡ there are also patterns for embroidery to be done upon a foundation of stuff with silks of various colours and gold and silver thread. Many embroidery stitches are mentioned, among others, *punto in aere*,§ a term afterwards

Madrid, a portrait of a woman, ascribed to Del Sarto (1486-1531), has a narrow edging of lace. Del Sarto's " Portrait of a Sculptor" (portrait of the artist) has a border of lace to the shirt (National Gallery). In Tintoretto (1518-1594) narrow lace, apparently bobbin-made, appears in the picture of " Lucretia."

* See Note, page 9.

† Esemplario di lavori, &c., N.D., Venice.

‡ Brunet gives an edition dated 1528.

§ In the six pages of instructions we learn the various stitches in which these wonderful patterns may be executed : " Damaschino, rilevato, a filo, sopra punto, ingaseato, Ciprioto, croceato, pugliese, scritto, incroceato, in aere, fatto su la rate, a magliato, desfilato, and di racammo" That *punto in aere* or *in aria* was a term used for embroidery appears from the fact that so early as " 1476 the Venetian Senate decreed that no *punto in aria* whatever, executed either in flax with a needle or in silver or gold thread, should be used on the curtains or bed-linen in the city or provinces."

Plate X.

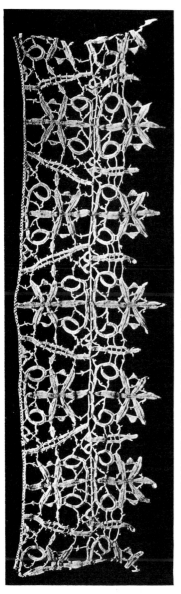

BORDER AND VANDYKE EDGE OF NEEDLEPOINT (*Punto in Aria*).
The pattern united by brides picotées.   Italian, early seventeenth century.

INSERTION OF RETICELLA.
Venetian, sixteenth century.

C

Plate XI.

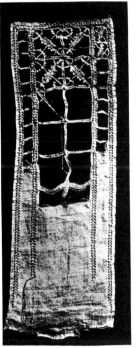

PIECE OF RETICELLA IN PROGRESS (Modern).

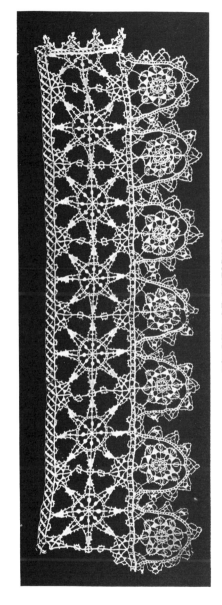

BORDER OF RETICELLA.

With Vandykes of *Punto in Aria.* Venetian, about 1580.

Plate XII.

PATTERN FOR RETICELLA.

With border of needlepoint.   From the pattern-book of Elisabetta Catanea Parasole, the "Teatro delle Nobili et Virtuose Donne," 1616.

used for needlepoint lace.   The designs to be worked for collars, bed-hangings, and insertions in pillow-cases consist of scrolls, arabesques, birds, animals, flowers, herbs, and grasses.

In fact all the earliest engraved pattern-books contain only designs for various sorts of embroidery upon material, such as darning upon canvas (*punto fa su la rete a maglia quadra*), drawn thread work of reticulated patterns (*punto tirato* or *punto a reticella*), and "cutwork" (*punto tagliato*)—cut-out linen, not the cutwork before described.

It is not until about thirty years later that we have special geo-metric patterns workable by lacemakers.   This development of lace was the consequence of the innovation of collars and ruffs, which began to be used in 1540.

From this date geometric lace made rapid progress, until it cul-minated in the beautiful and brilliant designs of Vinciolo (1587).*

* The various types of lace appear in the pattern-book of Elisabetta Catanea Parasole (1616).   Her patterns are entitled—(1) Merletti a piombini ; (2) Lavori di ponto reticella ; (3) Lavori di ponto reale e reticella (cutwork combined with reti-cella) ; (4) Lavori di ponto in aria.

CHAPTER IV.

Early Italian Bobbin Lace.

Knotted Fringes—Early Bobbin Lace (Merletti a Piombini)— Early Genoese Lace.

KNOTTING, a treatment of the fringed ends of stuff, may be considered a forerunner of bobbin lace, being made (when made separately as a fringe) on a pillow, though by knotting, and not by plaiting. A fringe of loose threads was formed at the edge of the material— generally linen—by drawing the warp threads, and then binding or knotting the weft threads together as tassels. During the sixteenth century much of this work was produced at Genoa. In a specimen illustrated in Elise Ricci's "Antiche trine Italiane," the threads are knotted to represent small figures. Macramé—a word of Arabic derivation used for a fringe or trimming—by which similar work is known in modern times, was reintroduced in Genoa in 1843.

The earliest bobbin lace appears in the form of twisted or plaited thread edgings for ruffs. Judging from the pattern-books in which they appear, they have the same dentated edge, but a more wiry make, and a lighter, more open appearance than the contemporary needle-points, and were consequently a more effective contrast to the lawn ruff.*

---

* "Ces guipures plus souples et plus vapeureuses que celles à l'aiguille, distribuées à flots au bord des enroulements de gaudrons à triple rang, donnaient à l'objet une certaine élégance qui rendait supportable son developpement exagéré; tandis que les passements de point coupé à l'aiguille, d'une nature plus ferme, fournissaient un pli plus sec dont les bords aigus, se tenant rangés trop correctement, les faisaient ressembler à une armée de piques qu'on aurait dites disposées pour la défensive" (Séguin, "La Dentelle").

Plate XIII.

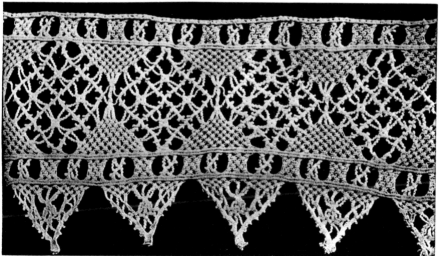

MACRAMÉ (Modern).

Plate XIV.

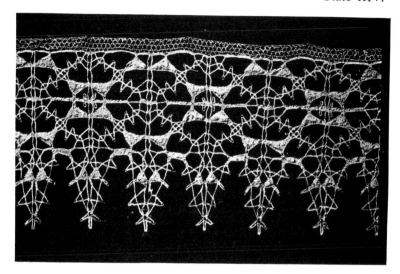

EARLY BOBBIN LACE.
Merletti a piombini.

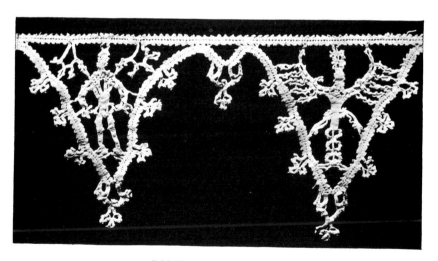

BOBBIN LACE (German).
In the possession of the Misses Trevelyan.

Plate XV.

COVERLET OF BOBBIN LACE (Italian).

In "Le Pompe" (1557) small round loops are shown at the edge of various details, and this ornament also appears in Parasole. It consists of a single thread brought out in a loop and carried back again. Larger loops of plaited thread are also used to give a light appearance to the pointed vandykes. The design is geometrical like cutwork, but the pattern is formed of *lines* rather than *solid forms*, and these lines are less rigid and precise than the more solid needle-point. A narrow "footing," though worked in with pattern, appears in many of these merletti a piombini.* The first edgings were narrow, and when a greater width was required the vandyked edge was sewn on to an insertion. The threads composing the pattern are, as has been said, plaited together, not worked across each other at right angles to form a linen-like toilé. The development of more important ornamental devices is shown in certain paintings, such as that of Charles of Saxony (1582), whose ruff is trimmed with deep and elaborate merletti a piombini.

Some later specimens show the transition from geometrical design to a conventional scroll with leafy ornaments. The important bed-cover in the Victoria and Albert Museum,† which is stated to be "either Flemish or Italian," and is catalogued under the Flemish laces, belongs to this period. To judge by the peculiar lightness and precision of the design, the "value" of the background, the design of the bordering pattern with its arrangement of diagonals with scrolling ends and the conventional treatment of every detail, it must be Italian, and probably Venetian (Plate XV.).

The piece is said to have belonged to Philip IV. of Spain, and the sixth circle from the centre is formed by the collar with jewels of the Golden Fleece, and within the four corners are two-headed eagles, displayed and surmounted by crowns.

* "*Merletti*, all manner of little battlements, also the several wards or springs in a lock, by met. long purles wrought in bone-laces, usually worn in bands or ruffs" (Dictionary of Florio and Torriano, London, 1659).

The Italian word for lace, *pizzi*, is also derived from the vandyked character of the early laces. "*Pizzetti*, tongs, languets, lappets, labels or latchets of anything, also peaks in bands and cuffs or any other linen" (Dictionary of Florio and Torriano, 1659).

"*Pizzo*, a peake or tip of anything" (Florio, "A Worlde of Wordes," 1598).

† No. 270, 1880.

The workmanship of this piece is remarkable. The plumage of the eagle is imitated by means of small holes left in the plaiting, in each of which a small loose loop or picot of thread appears. "The cross-bars of twisted threads which hold the feathers of the out-stretched wings in their places are separate details of twisting, and are looped into the edges of the feathers. This is also the case with the trellis-work which occupies the space between the central circular device and its square border." *

Genoa first imitated the gold threads of Cyprus, and her gold work, at first restricted to bed trimmings, was largely used for orna-menting dresses in the fifteenth century. After about 1420 this industry rapidly declined, and its workers emigrated. Genoese thread bobbin lace, which appears to have preserved the heaviness inseparable from metal passements, does not appear in portraits or inventories until just before the middle of the sixteenth century.† The portrait (Plate XVI.) of Henry II., Duc de Montmorency (d. 1632), one of the earliest examples, shows a deep and elaborate collar with a scalloped edge and wide insertion, and the popularity of Genoese lace was doubtless coincident with the first introduction of the falling collar, as it died out with the appearance of the cravat ‡ (about 1660).

Genoese lace, as has been said, was coarse and solid, a characteristic which is early noticed in the seventeenth-century *jeu-d'esprit*, known as " Revolte des Passemens," where it is spoken of as having " le corps un peu gros." This very heaviness and solidity was eminently suited to its use upon boot tops, garters, shoe-roses, carriages, as well as upon collars, scarves, aprons, &c.

The " wheat grain " § ornament reappears in the various examples, combined with vandykes of the usual plaited and twisted type. The

* Descriptive Catalogue of the Collections of Lace in the Victoria and Albert Museum, 1881.

† Vulson de la Colombière states that Genoese lace was not used in 1597.

‡ The cravat was a natural consequence of the periwig, which seems to have arisen in France about 1660. In England the Duke of York first wore one in 1663-4.

§ These " wheat-grains " are also a feature of Maltese lace. In 1833 Lady Hamilton Chichester introduced lace-making into Malta, and by adapting Genoese designs evolved what is known as Maltese lace by means of workers imported from Genoa.

Plate XVI.

PORTRAIT OF HENRI, DUC DE MONTMORENCY (1595-1632).
By Lenain.

D

Plate XVII.

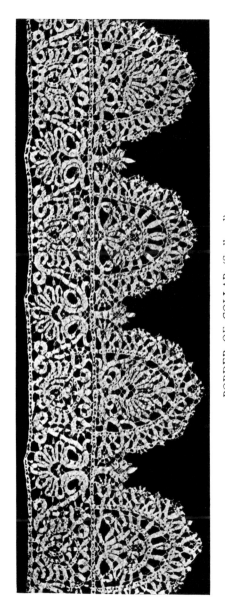

BORDER OF COLLAR (Scalloped).   Italian, early seventeenth century.

The narrow bands, twisted to form the ornament, are of plaited threads, a species of tape.

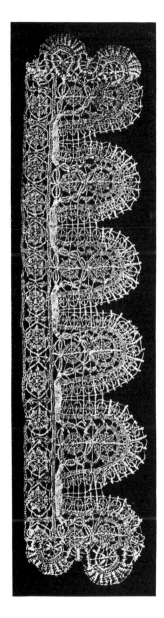

BOBBIN LACE.   Italian, early seventeenth century.

With round scallops.   Italian, early seventeenth century.

Plate XVIII.

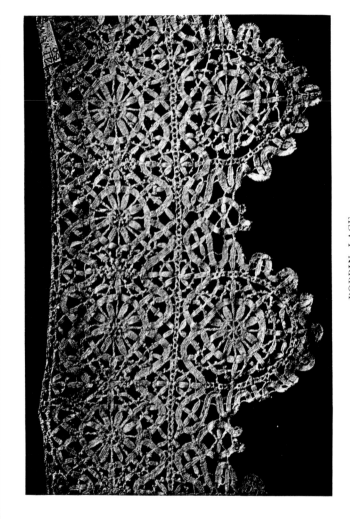

BOBBIN LACE.

With round scallops.   Genoese, early seventeenth century.

Plate XIX.

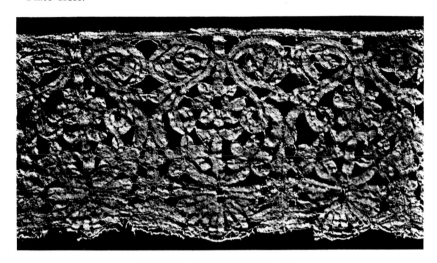

BOBBIN MADE TAPE-LACE.

The pattern is linked together by twisted threads.   Italian, seventeenth century.

ITALIAN TAPE-LACE.

With needlepoint fillings.   About 1640.

lace used to decorate the collars of the period appears to be of two distinct types: first, a scalloped lace (which was used contempor· aneously with the Flemish edgings for collars of the seventeenth century), the pattern of which consists of a tape-like, simple design, strengthened and connected by short brides. In the centre of the scallop is the profile of a flattened carnation. A succession of these carnation-like forms produces the effect of ornamental scallopings to the border. This lace was in vogue about 1640, succeeding the more formal scallops of the earlier part of the century.

The second type (point de Gênes frisé) is made entirely with plaits of four threads each, following the design, and is characterised by small oval enlargements resembling grains of wheat which are some-times arranged as beads on a thread and sometimes composed into trefoils and quatrefoils, or spokes radiating from a common centre (Plate XVIII.). This lace, made up of an insertion and an edging of deep rounded scallops, is well illustrated by Lenain in his portrait of Cinq Mars. The scalloped edge and the insertion were made separately, but were supposed to harmonise in pattern. In an early comedy of Corneille, "La Galerie du Palais," a character criticises a piece of point de Gênes, of which

> "la dentelle
> Est fort mal assorti avec le passement."

In the portrait of the Duc de Montmorency a figure of a horseman occurs in the insertion—an isolated example, for in no other illustra-tion or extant specimen has any deviation from simple geometrical design been introduced in point de Gênes frisé.*

By the middle of the seventeenth century the varieties of pillow lace had been considerably developed. The thin wiry pillow lace had been discarded, and the heavier Genoese collar laces went out of fashion, as we have said, by 1660. A tape lace with a straight edge between the ornament of which were grounds of meshes, or of bars or brides, was subsequently made in Genoa, and is remarkable for the twisting of the tape, always looped back upon itself.

---

* The name is an old one. In the wardrobe of Mary de Médicis is enumerated among other articles a "mouchoir de point de Gennes frisé" ("Garderobe de feue Madame," 1646 ; Bib. Nat. MSS., F. Fr. 11,426).

CHAPTER V.

VENETIAN NEEDLEPOINT AND BURANO LACE.

ACCORDING to Molmenti,* lace-making was always at Venice a private enterprise, unlike the great State-protected industries, such as the glass manufactures at Murano. A great quantity of cutwork was made in the houses of the nobility for their own use, and in the convents. Viena Vendramin Nani, to whom Vecellio dedicated his book † in 1591, was accustomed to make lace, and to employ the young women of her household in this "virtuous exercise."

Cutwork, as in France and England, was originally "greatly accepted of by ladies and gentlemen," and "consequently of the common people." The art spread downwards,‡ and in the time of Daru "occupait la population de la capitale"—the daughters of the fishermen in the islands and the convents, as Peuchet writes.§ Geometrical-patterned lace continued to be freely made for ornamenting linen for household purposes until the eighteenth century,‖ but in the

---

* "La Vie Privée à Venise."

† The "Corona delle nobili et virtuose donne" (1592). The dedication (dated 20th January 1591) is "Alla Clarissima et Illustrissima Signora Vendramina Nani," and mentions the delight she takes in these works and "in farne essercitar le donne di casa sua, ricetto delle piu virtuose giovani che hoggidi vivano in questa città."

‡ Morosini Grimani, wife of the Doge Marino Grimani, set up at her own expense a workshop, in which were employed 130 workwomen under the direction of a *mistra* (maestra), Cattarina Gardin, who worked exclusively for the Dogaressa.

§ "Dictionnaire Universel de la Géographie Commerçante," 1789.

‖ A piece of point lace border in white and brown thread, lent by Mrs C. Martin to the Victoria and Albert Museum, though of the eighteenth century, resembles the designs of the late sixteenth.

Plate XX.

LAVORO A PONTO IN ARIA.

DESIGN FOR PUNTO IN ARIA.

From the pattern-book of Elisabetta Catanea Parasole, the "Teatro delle Nobili et Virtuose Donne," 1616.

Plate XXI.

DESIGN FOR PUNTO IN ARIA.

From the pattern-book of Elisabetta Catanea Parasole, the "Teatro delle Nobili et Virtuose Donne," 1616.

Plate XXII.

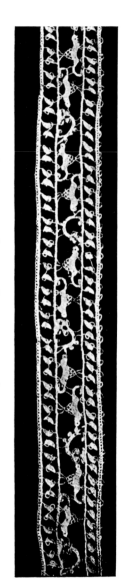

INSERTION OF NEEDLEPOINT LACE.

Venetian, late sixteenth or early seventeenth century. In the possession of Mrs J. H. Middleton.

INSERTION OF NEEDLEPOINT LACE.

last years of the sixteenth curved forms were introduced, and a new type of lace developed. In the early seventeenth century floral and human forms were often treated. The specimens with figures and animals are curious rather than beautiful. A type of lace of scroll design in flat needlepoint, recalling by its lightness very fine metal work or the arabesques of Persian ornament, is very interesting and well designed. In this type is a rosette-like or many-lobed flower, and the interlacing ribbon-like scrolls which show the influence of Oriental art. The solid part of the pattern is, in many cases, outlined by a slightly raised rib or edge, which also models portions of the ornament. The edge is also enriched by short picots, and the design is frequently united by short brides, either ornamented or varied by a single picot.

There is no distinguishing name for this rare and beautiful type of lace. It is, strictly speaking, *late punto in aria*, but the needle-point laces which were produced in the seventeenth and eighteenth centuries were virtually all comprised under the general name of *punto in aria*, for in 1616, 1633, and 1634, the Proveditori alle Pompe forbade the wearing of "punto in aere da Venezia," under penalty of a fine of two hundred ducats for each offence.

The term is an unfortunate one, as it was also applied to a stitch in embroidery,* "the high raised stitch," and continued to be applied to *every* kind of Venetian needlepoint lace. Marini quotes from a document of the seventeenth century, in which *punti in aria* appears to have been an alternative name for Burano lace,† and Peuchet states that Venetian laces were known by that name.‡

Rose point differs from *punto in aria* in three important details: in the highly conventional character of its design, its relief, and the elaboration of its brides. The design of the heavier rose points is

---

* *Punto in aria* in Florio and Torriano's Dictionary (1654) is defined as "the high raised stitch."

† "Elles portent le nom de point ou punti in aria" ("Dictionnaire Universel de la Géographie Commerçante," 1789).

‡ It is curious that in Florio's Dictionary the special terms used for lace have quite other significations. Pizzo is "a peake or tip of anything," Merli are "little turrets, spires, pinnacles, or battlements upon wals," Merletti, "the severall wards of a locke," Trine is a term for "cuts, iags, snips or such cuttings or pinching, pinkt works in garments." "Punto in aria" does not appear in Florio's "World of Wordes," 1598.

E

almost invariably a foliated scroll, with an ornamental flower based
upon the pomegranate, but much conventionalised. A natural pomegranate appears in many specimens of late *punto in aria*, but the
fruit, as it appears in rose point, is hardly recognisable. This conventional treatment of natural forms is a prominent feature of Italian
design, as compared with the more naturalistic art of France, Flanders,
and England.

Figures and natural objects are rarely introduced even in ecclesi-
astical lace. A specimen of rose point, however, illustrated in Elise
Ricci's "Antiche trine Italiane," shows a ship in sail containing three
figures ; and in a piece belonging to Mrs John Hungerford Pollen,
which forms the front opening of an alb, is represented the Madonna
crowned and seated on clouds, with her foot on the neck of a cherub,
and attired in a robe sprinkled with stars. Above are the Three
Persons of the Trinity. Part of the robes are worked in open stitch,
small black beads are added to the eyes. Mr Samuel Chick, again,
has an altar border, the central portion of which contains emblems of
the Passion. In the middle is our Lord's face upon a cushion wearing
the crown of thorns, and surmounted by a halo ; underneath are the
dice, pincers, flagellum, and hammer, to the right the flogging-post
and ladder, to the left the cross, spear, and sponge on a reed. At
the top are the crown of thorns and nails. This piece was at one
time the property of Mary of Orleans, Queen of Saxony, grand-
daughter of Charles I. of England.* In a curious "pale" or square
of rose point in the Victoria and Albert Museum (Plate XXXIII.),†
two angels are displayed holding up a chalice, above which is the
sacred monogram I.H.S. set in rays of glory. In one unique collar
mythological subjects are either outlined by pin-holes or distinguished
from the background by a closer stitch upon the flat toilé in irregular-
shaped compartments. In a triangular piece in the possession of
Mr Sydney Vacher stags and other conventionalised animals are
introduced. Such specimens, however, were no doubt experimental
in design, and are not often met with.

The second point in which rose point differs from *punto in aria*

* See Catalogue of the *Daily Mail* Exhibition of British Lace, March 1908.
† Victoria and Albert Museum, No. 556, 1875.

Plate XXIII.

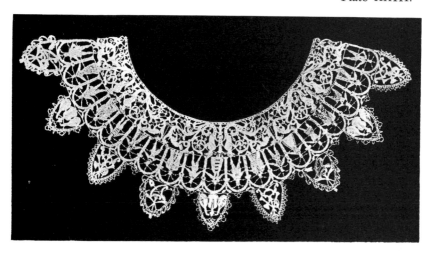

MODERN NEEDLEPOINT LACE.
After a design of Vecellio.

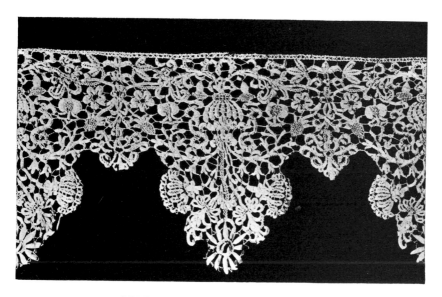

BORDER OF NEEDLEPOINT LACE.
With scallops. "Flat Venetian." In the possession of Mrs Christie Miller.

Plate XXIV.

COLLAR, ROSE-POINT.
Venetian, late seventeenth century.

Plate XXV.

PORTRAIT OF A MAN, SHOWING COLLAR OF ROSE-POINT.
French School. (*Corsini Gallery.*)

Plate XXVI.

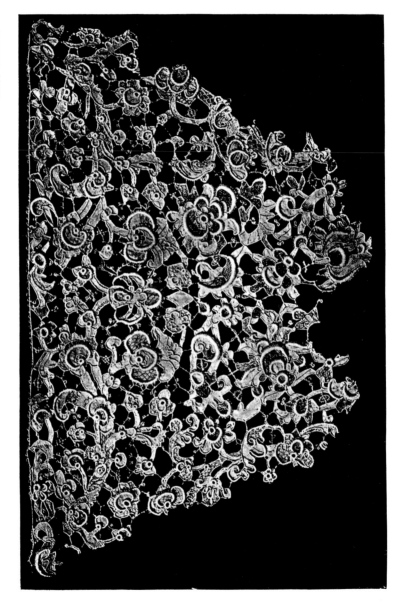

SPECIMEN OF PIECED ROSE-POINT.

Where detached flowers are joined into a mosaic without forming any consecutive pattern.

is in its relief. In rose point, besides the raised edge which it has in common with some specimens of flat Venetian,* higher relief is given by laying down a pad of coarse threads, varying according to the amount of relief it was desired to obtain, and covering this layer of thread by close button-hole stitches.

This thick sheaf of threads takes naturally an unbroken curve, and to this may be attributed the almost invariably rounded and lobed forms of the ornament. This pad is often ornamented with a close fringe of picots, or by an ornament of free loops — tier upon tier—ornamented with picots.

No open spaces or jours are introduced into the toilé, which is of an even and close button-hole stitch, varied by very small pin-holes arranged in lines or veins, or in simple chequer, chevron, or diamond diaper patterns, subordinated to the general effect of the design. In a specimen in the possession of Mr Sydney Vacher the pin-holes form a date.

The design is connected by a groundwork of brides, which have been already noticed in flat Venetian.

The brides, simple in the heavy points, become highly ornamented in the finest specimens, and in point de neige are ornamented not only with picots, but with picoted circles and semicircles, and S-shapes, and star devices. Sometimes the brides are single—sometimes two or three meet together, and are ornamented at the point of section †

* In some specimens of rose point, however, the pattern is not strengthened on the edge by outer cordonnets of button-hole stitched work.

† In three square inches of a very fine specimen of rose point the following varieties of brides are to be found :—(1) A single bride ornamented with picots. (2) Double brides joined in the centre and ornamented at the sides by a circle four times picoté. Small picots also ornament the brides between the circle and the extremities. (3) Three double brides meeting in a small triangle, each side of which is ornamented with a circle five times picoté. (4) Three brides meeting in a point in the centre. Each is ornamented in a different manner. The shortest bride is ornamented with two picots upon each side, and by two semicircles, joining the two other brides, and ornamented with six picots. The second bride is decorated at one end by a similar semicircle eight times picoté, which joins the semicircle previously described, thus forming an S-shaped figure. Upon the opposite side is a small semicircle ornamented with three picots, forming the head of the S. The third bride, at the point of intersection, is ornamented with a segment six times picoté, which forms the tail of the S. The foot of this bride

(Plate XXIX.). Occasionally there is a ground of cross-barring or trellis-pattern, the effect of which is a very open square mesh, ornamented at the points of section and in the centre of each side with an ornamented device or loop.

In certain late specimens the brides form a slightly irregular hexagonal mesh, richly picoté. This mesh is never, as in Argentan, a perfect hexagon, but is richer in effect, owing to this slight irregularity and to the enrichment of the picots, than the plain Argentan mesh.

The raised points are divided into gros point de Venise, punto neve (point de neige) with its ground of ornamented starred brides resembling snowflakes, and coraline point. Gros point de Venise, which was elaborated from 1620-50, and which was designed to lie flat and ungathered, is distinguished by the continuity of its designs, which are mostly horizontal; its scrolls are heavier than in point de neige, the brides simpler and less ornamental, the border or edge is usually straight—a single line of button-hole stitched thread enriched here and there with semicircles picoté. In point de neige, which was to hang fully or to be gathered, and which was in vogue from *circa* 1650-1720, the style is modified; the designs are composed on a smaller scale, and the groundwork of brides becomes a more important element, the scrolls are no longer continuous; detached sprays, consisting of slender leaves and minute renderings of the flowers of gros point, covered with a profusion of flying loops which almost hide the form it enriches, spring from a vase-like ornament and are arranged in many specimens symmetrically on either side of a vertical line. This change was probably owing to French influence.

is also ornamented with a small circle picoté. (5) A straight double bride ornamented at either end by two picots on either side, and in the centre by two semicircles joined, and connected by another semicircle, forming a trefoil. Each semicircle has three picots. (6) A double bride ornamented on either side by two picots; in the centre by two semicircles, each four times picoté. (7) Two single brides and one double bride meeting in a point, the single bride ornamented on one side by a semicircle four times picoté, the double bride ornamented in the centre with a circle four times picoté. At the point of section the three brides are united by three semicircles five times picoté, forming a rosette. (8) Three curved brides meeting in a point, each bride being ornamented by a scroll-shaped ornament which crosses it, and ornamented with thirteen picots.

Plate XXVII.

COLLAR COMPOSED LARGELY OF CUT LINEN, TO IMITATE ROSE-POINT.

Plate XXVIII.

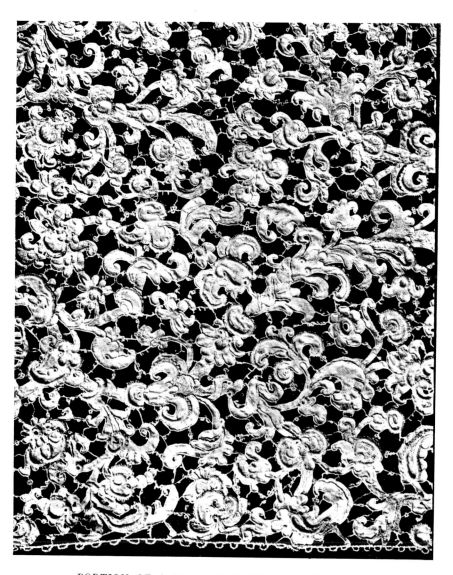

PORTION OF A WIDE FLOUNCE OF ROSE-POINT.

F

Plate XXIX.

PORTION OF A FLOUNCE OF FINE ROSE POINT.
Venetian, early eighteenth century.

Plate XXX.

UNFINISHED PIECE OF LACE. German, eighteenth century.

Tacked on green paper. Made by Frau M. v. Vislinghoff at Freiburg.

S-shaped motifs are frequent, and upon details of the pattern knot-work is used as ornament. This type is always ornamented with a hanging pattern, or one in which the arrangement of the details is conspicuously vertical, which was more appropriate to the folds of cravats and full flounces than are the horizontal and continuous scrolls of the gros point de Venise.

Coraline point is a very attenuated variety of rose point in which relief is almost entirely absent, the leaves of the scroll have entirely disappeared, leaving a winding tangle of narrow coral-like ramifications ending in a small unimportant flower. The ground is of brides picotées arranged in hexagonal meshes.

Point plat de Venise is similar in design to rose point, but, as its name implies, is entirely without relief. The diaper and chequer pin-hole patterns are more freely used than in rose point, but the general appearance is that of unfinished rose point.

It is to be borne in mind that much of this lace was the produce of private individuals, or of convents outside Italy, and similar designs were often interchanged ; but with the exception of such private or conventual manufactures of lace, it is highly improbable that point d'Espagne or Spanish point, a term applied to a heavier make of Venetian rose point, was ever made in Spain. The heavy and valuable point laces which unexpectedly came out of Spain after the dissolution of the monasteries in 1830, were in no way distinguishable from similar pieces known to be of Venetian workmanship, and it was no doubt from the great lace-making countries of Flanders and Italy that these valuable laces were brought.

From the unfinished piece of lace (Plate XXX.), made in the eighteenth century, at Freiburg, it will be seen that elaborate needle-point of typically Italian design was occasionally made outside Venice by private workers.

In point de Venise à réseau, a delicate type of Venetian needle-point, the design, unlike that of rose point which rarely varies from its variations on its highly ornamental flower, shows conventional tulips and pomegranates. This type of lace is chiefly distinguished by the conventional treatment and arrangement of the ornament, and by the general flat look of the work, by the outlining thicker thread or cordonnet stitched to the edges of the pattern and worked in flatly,* by a minute border to the cordonnet of small meshes which intervenes between it and the réseau, and by the horizontal appearance of the réseau, which is of square meshes composed of double-twisted threads throughout, and very fine. The pomegranate motif, so frequent in heavy rose point, reappears; but the crest of the fruit is elaborated into a scrolling leaf (Plate XXXVI.).

In other specimens a French influence is apparent in the larger number of open modes, in the ribbon motif crossing the design, the spacing of the ornament, and the cordonnet which is worked around certain flowers, and the more broken outlines of the ornament.

The work of these grounded laces is always flat; but in some pieces minute raised button-hole stitched rings are added.

Compared with this type, Brussels could not reach the high standard of Venetian workmanship, being forced to content herself with a frequent use of modes more open than the fine close modes belonging to the Venetian point à réseau, which are in general bar, chevron, trellis, and chequer pin-hole patterns, such as are found in the raised points. Variety of effect is obtained by the use of barring (or honey-comb grounding) inserted amongst the stems and leaves of the sprays; but very open modes, as a general rule, are used sparingly, like "high lights" upon a picture. The style of Venetian à réseau is less floral and more conventional than in Brussels; and the cordonnet of Brussels straggles.

From this grounded point certain details of fine Alençon appear to have been borrowed. Alençon differs from grounded Venetian point in design. Whatever France touched became French. Naturalistic imitations of flowers, birds, vases, and other material objects are freely interspersed in the more ornamental portions of Alençon, while in Venetian lace there is rarely any change from purely conventional treatment. Alençon also differs in workmanship from Venetian point in the raised and continuous outlines to the ornament. Lighter and more open decorative modes are introduced in Alençon; the réseau rosacé (v. p. 68) is more freely used as a groundwork; the réseau of grounded Venetian point is square; that of Alençon is hexagonal and

---

* In some specimens certain details are outlined with a thick thread stitched along the stems, leaves, and flowers. The introduction of the thick thread, to give stronger definition to some of the forms, is, however, unusual in this make of lace.

Plate XXXI.

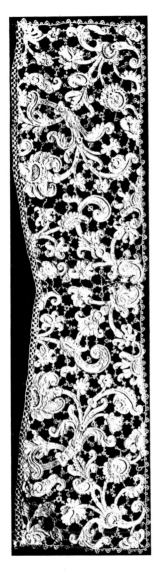

ROSE-POINT.

Venetian, late seventeenth or early eighteenth century.

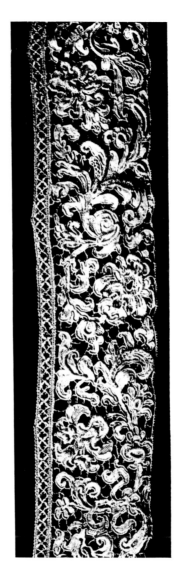

PORTION OF BORDER OF ROSE POINT.

With highly raised and padded ornament. Probably Spanish.

Plate XXXII.

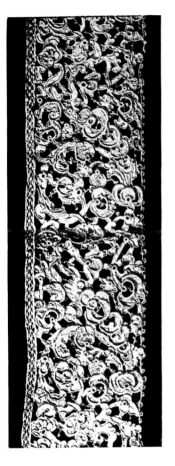

PORTION OF BORDER OF ROSE POINT.

Of crowded design, and with few brides, but perfect, as the pattern repeats, and the curve of the scroll is not forced.

PIECE OF GREEN PARCHMENT.

Showing needlepoint lace partially worked.

Plate XXXIII.

ROSE-POINT SQUARE.

A pale for covering the paten. The design displays two angels holding up the chalice,
above which is the sacred monogram I.H.S. Rose point, seventeenth century.
The details of the ornament are pieced.

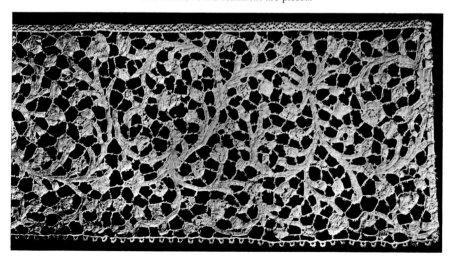

FLAT NEEDLEPOINT.

less fine ; the horizontal waved lines of the réseau are more irregular and marked in Alençon ; the foliations in point de Venise à réseau are marked by minute regular open-worked fibres or veinings.

In general appearance, according to Mr Cole, the designs would seem to give a date somewhere about 1650, that is, at the time when the raised points were largely in circulation. Upon the establishment of the Points de France, in 1665, the French were diligent under the tuition of their Venetian workers in their attempts to imitate. Upon this the skill and invention of the Venetians perfected the point à réseau—an attempt to win back the custom the French manufacturers were taking away from them. Here their labours culminated. As Alençon rose this type of lace declined. "Hence it is that point de Venise à réseau, having probably had but a short existence, died out soon; comparatively few specimens of it are to be seen." There are a fair number of specimens in perfect preservation—the Victoria and Albert Museum is peculiarly rich in them—and these do not appear to be later than the last years of the seventeenth and the beginning of the eighteenth century. At the beginning of the eighteenth century the lace industry was already declining. In 1734, French, Flemish, and English laces were sold at cheaper rates in the Venetian lace shops than the local production.*

In 1750, Benedetto Raniari and Pietro Gabriele attempted to " improve" the lace industry by imitating Flemish and French laces, especially blonde. They were exempted from taxation for ten years by the Senate, and their enterprise succeeded from the commercial, if not from the artistic, standpoint, as is proved by their prosperity in 1758.†

The old Burano laces are a coarser outcome of the point de

---

* " Figurarsi lo Stato Veneto tributario degli Stati forestieri nell' industria dei pizzi. E'l bello è che verso la metà del xviii. secolo alcune botteghe veneziane vendevano per lo piu de' pizzi esteri. Nel 1734 existevano ancora a Venezia i seguenti spacci de pizzi : al San Carlo, alle due Rose, all Premio, all Bucintor Ducale, all' Aquila d'oro, alla Madonna degli Angeli, al Cardinal. Non pochi certamente e più che sufficienti se in ognuno se fosse lavorato e venduto soltando della produzion locale " (Melani, " Svaghi Artistici Femminili").

† " Nel 1758, si racconta, erano addette alla suddetta fabbricia quindici maestre e quattrocentotrentetre scolari e in dicci anni vi si produssono 289,000 braccia di pizzi di varia altezza " (Ibid.).

Venise à réseau, and alone of all the Venetian needle laces survived the dark days of the close of the eighteenth century. Marini quotes from a document of the seventeenth century in which, speaking of merletti, it is said that "these laces, styled 'punti in aria,' or di Burano, because the greater part of them were made in the country so called, are considered by Lannoni as more noble and of greater whiteness, and for excellency of design and perfect workmanship equal to those of Flanders, and in solidity superior."

Very little is known of the early history of Burano lace. Peuchet* writes that a great number of fisherfolk in the island of Burano, as well as people in Venice itself and in the convents, were employed in lace-making ; but that their profits were small. The thread, he adds, comes from Flanders, as the local flax thread was not so strong when equally fine. In 1793 the *Gazetta Veneta* refers to Burano lace, "del quale si exercitava largo commercio anche nei vecchi tempi." †

The designs of old Burano, like those of Venise à réseau, are distinguished by a conventional treatment of the flowers and ornament ; but the designs are somewhat thinner, there is more réseau in proportion to the pattern, and in some specimens there are semés upon the ground, as in French laces of the Louis XVI. period.

In a description in a letter written in 1875, of certain Burano laces in the possession of Sir Henry (then Mr) Layard, specimens were described as "exactly like Alençon," ‡ the only difference perceptible being that "the flowers are matted and thick, and very clumsily put into the ground." In an account of Venetian lace-making, written by

---

* "Dictionnaire Universel de la Geógraphie Commerçante," 1789.

† Melani, "Svaghi Artistici Femminili." "Il Moschini nel suo 'Itineraire' mostro che nel 1819 nell' isola de Burano non era scomparsa ancora l'industria dei pizzi" (*Ibid.*).

‡ Extract from a letter of 30th August 1875, to Mr A. Blackborne, *re* Burano laces : "Lady Layard joined with Sir Henry Layard in this enterprise, but it was not successful. Modern Burano laces at first suffered from the quality of the thread." One disadvantage long seemed unsurmountable, the coarseness and unevenness of any thread that would then be found in Italy. This difficulty, which had so much to do with the failure of the English lace trade in the seventeenth century, threatened to doom modern Burano lace to an inevitable inferiority. However, thread was chosen by Baron Beckmann, imported from the Belgian thread manufacturers, and much improved the quality of lace produced.

Plate XXXIV.

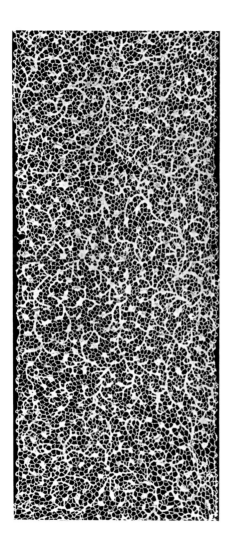

CORALINE POINT.

Italian, late seventeenth or first half of eighteenth century.

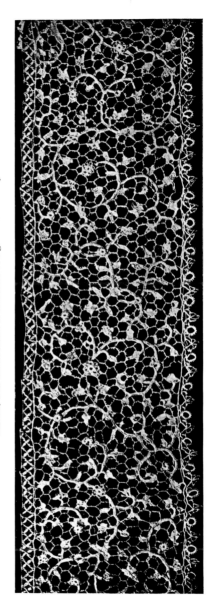

TRANSITIONAL PIECE BETWEEN ROSE AND CORALINE POINT.

Plate XXXV.

POINT DE VENISE À RÉSEAU.
Eighteenth century.

POINT DE VENISE À RÉSEAU.
First half of eighteenth century.

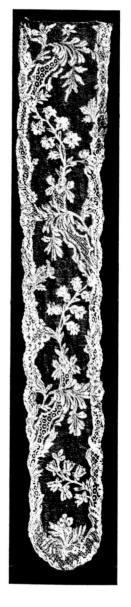

LAPPET OF POINT DE VENISE À RÉSEAU.
End of seventeenth century.

G

Plate XXXVI.

LAPPET OF POINT DE VENISE À RÉSEAU.

First half of eighteenth century.

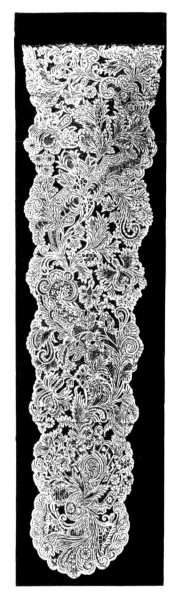

LAPPET OF POINT DE VENISE À RÉSEAU.

First half of eighteenth century.

Urbani de' Gheltof, published in Venice, and translated into English by Lady Layard, a very detailed description, accompanied by diagrams, is given of the mode of execution of Burano point.

From this it appears that it is usually worked on a pillow, not, however, of course with bobbins, as for bobbin lace, the object of the pillow or bolster is merely to raise the work to a suitable height on the lap of the lace-maker, and to diminish the necessity of much handling. On the middle of the upper side of the pillow there rests a small wooden cylinder across which the parchment pattern is stretched, leaving an open space under it for the convenience of the worker ; thus the strip of lace is kept smooth and flat. In working the réseau ground, a thread is fixed straight across the whole width of the lace as a foundation of each row of meshes, being passed through and fastened to any sprig or part of the pattern which may intervene, and on this thread the looped meshes are worked. The result is the formation of a remarkably square-shaped mesh, and by this and also by the streaky and cloudy appearance of the réseau (owing to the bad quality and unevenness of the thread), Burano point may be recognised. The cordonnet is, like the Brussels needlepoint,* of thread stitched round the outline, instead of the Alençon button-hole stitch over horsehair.

In 1866 the industry was extinct.† "Venice point," writes Mrs Palliser, " is now no more ; the sole relic of this far-famed trade is the coarse torchon lace of the old lozenge pattern, offered by the peasant women of Palestrina to strangers on their arrivals at hotels."

* Sometimes the cordonnet is button-hole stitched.

† An important revival of the Burano industry took place after the great distress following the severe winter of 1872. The Burano workers do not copy only the old Burano lace, but laces of almost any design or model.

CHAPTER VI.

MILANESE LACE.

MILAN, like many another centre of lacemaking, was early famed for its embroideries.* In 1584 a "Università" of embroiderers was already in existence, and flourished until the middle of the seventeenth century. Coryat mentions that the Milanese embroiderers are "very singular workmen, who work much in gold and silver." In the Sforza Visconti Inventory, the well-known instrument of partition between the sisters Angela and Ippolita Sforza Visconti,† are to be found the earliest records which are quoted in reference to Italian lace. *Trina* is mentioned there under its old form *tarnete*, but trina, like our English "lace" and the French "passement," was used in a general sense for braid or passement long before the advent of lace proper. Florio, in his Dictionary (1598), gives *trine*, cuts, tags, snips, pinck worke on garments, and *trinci*, gardings, fringings, lacings, &c. It will be seen that the "trine" of the Sforza Inventory are always of metal and silk.

---

* Brantôme, in his "Dames Galantes," remarks that the embroiderers of Milan "ont sceu bien faire par dessus les autres."

† "Lenzuolo (sheet) uno di revo di tele (linen thread), cinque lavorato a punto.

"Peza de tarnete (trina) d'argento facte a stelle.

"Lenzolo uno de tele, quatro lavorate a radexelo.

"Peza quatro de radexela per mettere ad uno moscheto (zanzariere—mosquito curtain).

"Tarneta uno d'oro et seda negra facta da ossi (bones).

"Pecto une d'oro facto a grupi.

"Binda una lavorata a poncto de doii fuxi (two bobbins?) per uno lenzolo" ("Instrumento di divizione tre le sorelle Angela ed Ippolita Sforza Visconti, di Milano, 1493, giorno di Giovedì, 12 Settembre").

Plate XXXVII.

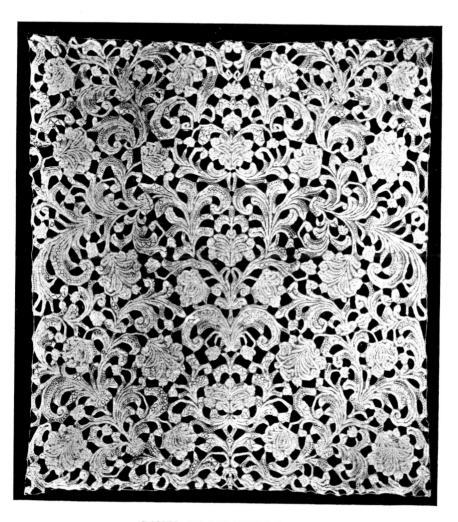

PANEL OF MILANESE LACE.

Without brides.   Seventeenth century.

Plate XXXVIII.

BORDER OF MILANESE LACE.
About 1650-60.

BORDER OF MILANESE LACE.
With brides. Seventeenth century.

Plate XXXIX.

PORTION OF A BORDER OF MILANESE LACE.

With réseau ground.   Late seventeenth century.   (*In the possession of Mrs Hibbert.*)

Plate XI.

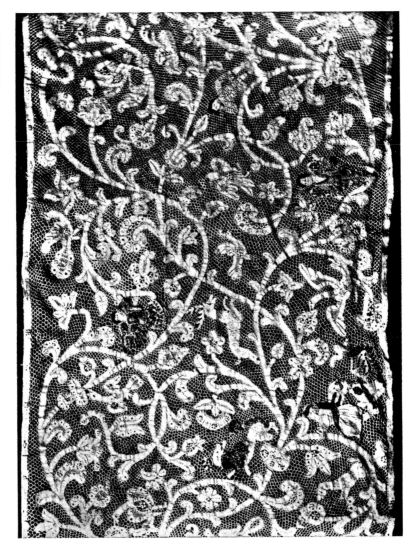

PORTION OF A BORDER OF MILANESE LACE.

With réseau ground. Late seventeenth century. (*In the possession of Mrs Hibbert.*)

Frattini, in his "Storia dell' Industria Manufatturiera in Lombardia," states the inhabitants of the Cantu district made lace from about 1600. Towards the middle of the eighteenth century the industry had fallen into decay. "The Milanese," writes Lalande, "only fabricate lace of an inferior quality," * to which may be added the later testimony of Peuchet, who writes that the laces are very common and not highly priced.†

The earlier Milanese laces are not grounded with the réseau, but covered by bold rolling scroll designs held together by brides, sometimes of twisted strands of thread. A specimen in the Bolckow Bequest, catalogued as Italian or Flemish, but certainly Italian in treatment, has a design of large flowering scrolls, in the centre of which is a lady playing a lute, while toward her flies a cupid bearing a heart, and on the other side is a nude figure with a flowing scarf. The cupid, blindfolded, has a bow and arrows (Plate XXXVIII.). One very fine piece of Milanese lace in the Victoria and Albert Museum has no brides; the details of the pattern touch one another ‡ (Plate XXXVII.). The toilé is a close, firm, even braid, varied with pin holes, or larger open devices. The réseau ground was introduced by 1664, at which date a portrait by Gonzales Coques shows a straight-edged piece of Milanese with meshed ground.

The réseau is of various kinds. Its most common type is a diamond-shaped mesh, formed with a plait of four threads like Valenciennes, but many experimental grounds, loosely worked, are met with in earlier pieces. Sometimes the mesh is square with the threads knotted at the points of intersection.

The pattern is first made on the pillow by itself, and the réseau ground is worked in round it afterwards, sloping in all directions so as to fit the spaces, while Valenciennes is worked all in one piece,

* "Voyage en Italie," 1765.

† "Milan. Dentelles en fil.—Elles sont très-communes. Cette fabrique n'a rien qui puisse nuire aux fabriques françaises de même espèce, ni pour la concurrance ni pour la consommation de Milan. Beaucoup sont employées par les paysannes de la Lombardie. La plus fine peut procurer quelque manchettes d'hommes d'un prix fort modique" ("Dictionnaire Universel de la Géographie Commerçante," 1789).

‡ No. 42, 1903.

pattern and réseau together. If the lace is turned upon the wrong side the strands of thread of the Milanese réseau can be seen carried behind the pattern. The designs are beautiful, and consist of light ribbon-like scrolls and conventional flowers,* which enclose small chequer or other simple fillings. Animal forms, eagles, hares, bears, hounds, archaic in drawing, but always vigorously treated, are frequently introduced.

Coats of arms are frequently met with, and animals which, no doubt, represent family badges. The double or imperial eagle is of very common occurrence. This is to be accounted for by the fact that Charles V. conceded as a mark of special favour the privilege of bearing the imperial arms to several Italian as well as Spanish families, who used them instead of their own arms.†

The very curious piece of Milanese lace (Plates XXXIX. and XL.), shows a clumsily-drawn figure seated upon an ornamental fountain. The graceful scrolls include various long-tailed birds, angels, horsemen chasing stags and lions ; while part of the pattern has a kind of knot-work upon the more important motifs ; the lion's mane, the angel, the horsemen are ornamented with this work in black silk, as is also the double eagle surmounted by a crown. It is dated 16..5.

In church lace, figures of the Virgin, angels, and monograms occur.

An interesting piece, dated 1733, in the Musée des Arts Décoratifs, at Brussels (of which two photographs are given on Plate XLIII.), should be studied. The first portion, with arms of " Julius Cæsar Xaverius Miccolis abbas et rector S. Mariæ Græcæ, A.D. 1733," and its repeating scroll design with its characteristic birds and stags is perfect, while the second portion shows a hopeless confusion of motifs carelessly thrown together, and the réseau mended. The angels supporting the shield with its rayed monstrance are followed by a stag and a crowned double eagle, which are quite unrelated to the design and to each other. The scroll, instead of repeating like the first portion, is twisted into a broken and irregular volute, and a single

---

* Not conventional beyond recognition, like these highly ornamental flowers of Venetian rose point. The pink, lily, and other flowers are met with, often treated naturalistically.

† From 1535 till 1714 Milan was a dependency of the Spanish Crown.

Plate XLI.

BORDER OF MILANESE LACE.
With réseau ground.

Plate XLII.

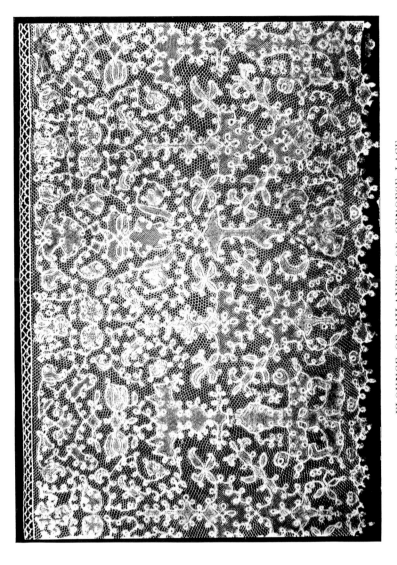

FLOUNCE OF MILANESE OR GENOESE LACE.

Late eighteenth century. (*In the possession of the Misses Trevelyan.*)

Plate XLIII.

BORDER OF MILANESE LACE.
Dated 1733.

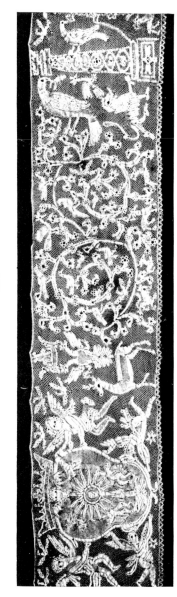

BORDER OF MILANESE LACE.
Dated 1733.

Plate XLIV.

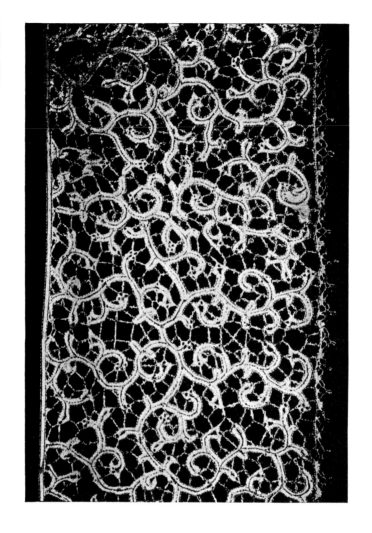

BORDER OF MILANESE OR GENOESE LACE.

Late eighteenth century.

supporter of the abbot's arms is transferred to a new position beside
an ornamental pillar.

Plate XLI., with its naïve rendering of floral design, is perhaps a
late or peasant rendering of Milanese work ; the twisting, ribbon-like
convolutions, which may be seen in the stems of the flowers and other
ornament, became more prominent in the decadence of Milanese lace.
The trade name for such lace is " Genoese lace," but it was made both
in Milan and Genoa and the district. The design consists merely of
the tape looping back upon itself, and linked together by brides with
picots, or with a réseau ground. It has been much used for church
vestments, and was frequently of considerable width (Plate XLII.).

Strong peasant bobbin laces were made very freely throughout
the seventeenth and eighteenth centuries in Northern Italy. Coryat *
notices in Piedmont "that many of the inns have white canopies and
curtains made of needlework, which are edged with very fine bone-
lace," and in Venice that "the sides under the benches" in the
gondolas are "garnished with fine linen cloth, the edge whereof is
laced with bone-lace." About fifty years ago, sheets and pillow-cases,
towels and table-cloths were still to be bought from country inns,
trimmed with pillow lace of coarse thread and indeterminate pattern.

* Coryat's Crudities, 1611.

36

CHAPTER VII.

CRETAN.

BOBBIN-LACE making in Crete would seem to have arisen in consequence of Venetian intercourse with the island,* and Cretan white thread laces bear distinct traces of Venetian influence, as for example those in which costumed figures are introduced. " As a rule, the motives of Cretan lace patterns are traceable to orderly arrangement and balance of simple geometric and symmetrical details, such as diamonds, triangles, and quaint polygonal figures, which are displayed upon groundworks of small meshes. The workmanship is somewhat remarkable, especially that displayed in the making of the meshes for the grounds. Here we have an evidence of ability to twist and plait threads as marked, almost, as that shown by lace-makers of Brussels and Mechlin. Whether the twisting and plaiting of threads to form the meshes in this Cretan lace was done with the help of pins or fine pointed bones, may be a question difficult to solve." † Cretan lace is very often worked on silk. The patterns in the majority of the specimens made of linen thread are outlined with one, two, or three bright coloured silken threads, which may have been run in with a needle.

* In the partition of the Greek Empire after the capture of Constantinople by the Latins in 1204, Crete fell to the lot of Boniface, Marquis of Montferrat, and was by him sold to the Venetians, to whom it continued subject for more than four centuries, till 1669.

† " A Descriptive Catalogue of the Collections of Lace in the Victoria and Albert Museum."

Plate XLV.

FLEMISH OR BELGIAN LACE.

Seventeenth century. Known as " Bruges."

37

CHAPTER VIII.

FLANDERS.

WHILE the conditions of art in Flanders—wealthy, bourgeois, proud and free—were not dissimilar to those of the art of Venice, from the very infancy of Flemish art an active intercourse was maintained between the Low Countries and the great centres of Italian art, so that it was not unnatural that at the close of the sixteenth century laces were known and made in Flanders.* As a matter of fact, Flemish paintings do not begin to show the use of lace until about 1600.† The evidence of the series of engravings after Martin de Vos is hardly conclusive as to the making of bobbin lace in Flanders in the sixteenth century, as he spent many years in Italy; and though the third of the series (assigned to the *age mûr*) shows a girl sitting with a pillow on her knees making bobbin-lace, the treatment and the background are Italian.

Needlepoint lace was hardly made at all. A specimen of needlepoint lace, of which the pattern consists of a number of small blossom devices arranged very closely together, is notable for the characteristic absence of contrast between the compactly worked ornaments and

---

* "It is a noteworthy circumstance that the two widely distant regions of Europe where pictorial art first flourished and attained a high perfection, North Italy and Flanders, were precisely the localities where lace-making first took root and became an industry of importance both from an artistic and from a commercial point of view" (Art. *Lace*, Encyclopædia Britannica).

† "I ritratti fiamminghi non cominciano a essere ornati di pizzi che intorno al 1600; solo dopo il 1600 l'uso di cotale ornamento e estesissimo nelle Fiandre" (A. Melani, "Svaghi Artistici Femminili").

open spaces about them, and the same defect is to be seen in Flemish bobbin laces of the same period.*

In the Wardrobe Accounts of Queen Elizabeth, Flanders cutwork is priced less highly than the Italian variety and is of less frequent occurrence.†

In one point Flanders was superior to other countries of Europe— its linen, whereof the Flemish "exporte great quantity, and fyner then any other part of Europe yealdeth."‡ Spinning flax threads and weaving fine textiles is closely associated with the early commercial history of Flanders, and "when the progress of manufactures was endangered by the religious persecutions of the sixteenth century, the linen trade alone is said to have upheld itself, and to have saved the country from ruin." The fineness of the thread used especially affected the lace designs when the early twisted and plaited merletti a piombini after the Italian models began to give way to scalloped laces in which flattened, broader tape-like lines forming some sort of floral ornament, were prominent.§ These date from about 1630 to 1660. Curved forms seem to have been found easy of execution in the bobbin lace, no doubt because (unlike reticella) it was not constrained by a foundation of any sort.

The immense quantity of bobbin lace produced in Flanders during the seventeenth century was aided by the improvements in spinning threads,‖ and in the making of pins.

The design, as we have said, is usually somewhat crowded,¶ com-

---

* Victoria and Albert Museum, No. 243, 1881.

† "For one yard of double Italian cutwork, a quarter of a yard wide, 55s. 4d. For one yard of double Flanders cutwork, worked with Italian purl, 33s. 4d." (G.W.A., 33rd and 34th Elizabeth).

‡ Fynes Moryson.

§ About 1630. A portrait of a lady by Rembrandt about 1640, in the Royal collection at Windsor Castle, shows a fichu bordered with scallops of this type of lace.

‖ The first improvement in the primitive spindle was found in the construction of the hand-wheel, in which the spindle mounted in a frame, was fixed horizontally and rotated by a band passing round it and a large wheel set in the same framework. Such a wheel became known in Europe about the middle of the sixteenth century.

¶ "While the painters of Germany and the Netherlands were fond of filling a given space with figures and incidents, the Italians preferred to deal with an

Plate XLVI.

FLEMISH LACE.
Late seventeenth century.

Plate XLVII.

FLEMISH LACE.
Beginning of the eighteenth century.

posed of the local flora;* the edge spread into a fan-shaped or rounded broad scallop. In Flanders a means was invented for producing laces of great width, which consisted of "dividing the patterns not by bands, but into small and separate pieces, the boundaries of which coincided with the capricious curves of the ornament."

Of this century is a bobbin-made lace à brides—"point de Flandres," or "guipure de Flandres" as it is sometimes called. In this the pattern is composed of bold scrolling stems connected together by brides à picots. When the ground to lace of similar character and make consisted of small meshes, the lace was termed point d'Angleterre, and was made for the English market.†

There has been some doubt as to the country of origin of certain seventeenth-century pillow-made tape guipures in the Victoria and Albert Museum, which are described in the cases containing them as "Flemish or Italian." If a distinctive difference may be suggested between lace of the same style of pattern made in the two countries, it would perhaps appear to be in the quality of the thread. As has been said, the inhabitants of the Flemish provinces have always been noted for their superior skill in spinning and weaving linen, and from a difference in national taste, Italian lace is heavier and stouter than that produced in the north of Europe. The loose texture of this Flemish lace gives a pulled appearance to the outline, as if the brides were slightly straining it, and the pin-holes, from the same looseness, appear less precise in form than in the Italian work.

Pillow-tape guipure is composed of a tape made on the pillow to follow the curves of the pattern, and connected by brides, generally plaited, also made on the pillow, or by "sewings."

---

expanse of background, and by their treatment of it, gave an effect of air and freedom to the scene" (Woltmann and Woermann, "History of Painting," p. 399).

* "Pour la plupart de la nationalité germaine, les populations du nord-ouest de la Gaule tiennent de cette origine des tendances vers le naturalisme dans l'art. Cette origine a contribué . . . à donner aux habitants de la Gaule Belgique, comme trait principal de leur physiognomie artistique, une aptitude toute speciale à reproduire la nature" (Deshaisnes, " Histoire de l'Art dans la Flandre").

† For explanation of this name, see p. 48 *et seq.*

The braid follows the curves and lines of the pattern, and the various turns and curves are connected by means of sewings. The manner in which the braid is carried round the curves is extremely ingenious. By working partly across the braid and then returning to the outer edge of the curve a kind of wedge can be formed which brings the work round flat without any apparent thickening of the material. In the Flemish lace the fine thread obviated the necessity for the careful turning of the curves, and the method was gradually forgotten. Though we see less of the absolutely continuous line, patterns remained of a continuous scrolling character.

The "sewing" (as now practised by Brussels lace workers) is formed by catching a thread through a pin-hole in an adjacent piece of braid, and passing another thread through the loop thus formed. In this way a pattern worked in separate narrow lines is all joined into a homogeneous whole. Sometimes instead of the braids being closely united, two threads are twisted, or four threads are plaited into a bride fastened with a sewing into a part of the pattern, and then carried back into the braid.

In most of the pillow guipures the braid is lightened by holes or "bird's eyes," sometimes single, sometimes arranged in groups. Sometimes a coarse quality of lace was made in which tape (not the tape made on the pillow) was used. The weaving of tape appears to have been begun in Flanders about the end of the sixteenth or the beginning of the seventeenth century.

"Flat Spanish," or point de Flandres, is a pillow lace without any raised work. The lace was probably intended for Spanish consumption. "The making of lace," writes Sir John Sinclair in 1815, "at the time the French entered the Low Countries, employed a considerable number of people of both sexes. . . . A large quantity of sorted laces of a peculiar quality were exported to Spain and the colonies." The pattern which consists of detached and fantastic cut-up forms of varying widths, sprays, ribbons, flowers, &c., lightened by many varieties of open work, grillé, and veinings of pin-holes, &c., shows often an architectural and balanced arrangement.

A Flemish lace, straight-edged, with indeterminate pattern, and cloudy ground of irregular round circles with solid portions, is frequently met with. Its trade name is "Binche." Such specimens in

Plate XLVIII.

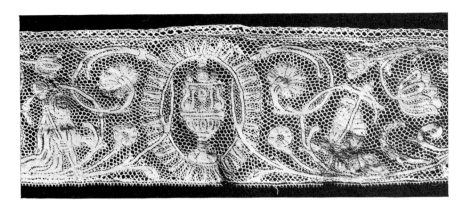

BORDER OF FLEMISH LACE.

With figures adoring a monstrance.

FLOUNCE OR BORDER OF FLEMISH (?) LACE.

Seventeenth century.

the Gruuthus Collection, however, as are attributed to Mechlin, in other collections are assigned to Antwerp. It is probable that it was a widely spread type of lace in Flanders, from which Mechlin, Valenciennes, &c., developed. It seems unlikely that this simple and ineffective lace was produced at Binche, of which the lace was admired by Savary, and said to be "equal to the laces of Brabant and Flanders."

CHAPTER IX.

BELGIAN LACE.

BRUGES LACE.

BRUGES made bobbin lace in the late seventeenth and early eighteenth centuries, and the name of Bruges is given to a lace of a scrolling character.* A guipure de Flandres piece of this kind, dated 1684, is preserved at Bruges, in the Chapelle du Saint Sang. The central portion shows two angels supporting the tube of the Holy Blood.† This oblong picture is surrounded by a scrolling design upon a réseau ground.

There is a good collection in the Gruuthus Museum, and a number of pieces were given to the Victoria and Albert Museum by the Rev. R. Brooke. The earlier examples have no brides; the later have brides picotées. The pattern as a rule resembles that of Venetian rose point. It is interesting to notice the pillow renderings of forms of "diaperings" and modes, which were originally done with the needle.

Later than the ground of brides is the réseau, of which there are some good specimens in the Victoria and Albert Museum. One specimen shows the tendency to naturalistic treatment of flowers in the eighteenth century, and has its floreated scroll pattern ornamented with tulips, primulas, and poppy-pods, acorns, &c.‡

---

* Société de l'Art ancien en Belgique, 1883-92.

† A copy in lace of the original glass tube containing the Holy Blood, which, though broken, is still preserved in the chapel.

‡ No. 888, 1853.

Plate XLIX.

SQUARE OF BRUSSELS LACE.
Early eighteenth century.

BRUSSELS LACE.

There is at present no information as to the date when the manufacture of Brussels lace began. In the eighteenth century it was famous, as Lord Chesterfield wrote in 1741, as the place "where most of the fine laces are made you see worn in England." The Béguinage was a great centre for lace-making, and English travellers often visited to buy lace.* In 1756 a Mrs Calderwood, who visited it, gave an account of the process of lace-making. "The manufacture is very curious," she writes; "one person works the flowers. They are all sold separate, and you will see a very pretty sprig for which the worker only gets twelve sous. The masters who have all these people employed give them the thread to make them; this they do according to a pattern, and give them out to be grounded; after which they give them to a third hand, who 'hearts' all the flowers with the open-work. That is what makes the lace so much dearer than the Mechlin, which is wrought all at once."† Thus half-way through the eighteenth century some special characteristics of Brussels work—the low rate of wages, the division of labour, and the *specialisation* of lace-workers on some branch of this work, the domination of the "masters"—is already established.

Brussels pillow lace is, as Mrs Calderwood writes, not made in one piece on the pillow; the réseau ground is worked in round the pattern which has been *separately* made.‡ "Thus the long threads that form the toilé of Brussels lace of all dates always follow the curves of the patterns, while in other Flemish laces these strands are found to run parallel to the edge the whole length of the lace, and *to pass* through the pattern into the réseau ground."§

* "We went to the Béguinage Convent to buy lace" (Letter of Elizabeth Viscountess Nuneham, 1766—"Harcourt Papers," vol. xi.).

† "Mrs Calderwood's Journey through Holland and Belgium, 1756" (printed by the Maitland Club).

‡ In old Brussels lace the ornament was worked on the pillow into the ground. Later, and at the present time, the flowers are applied to or sewn in the ground. Sometimes they are sewn on to the ground.

§ A. M. S., "Point and Pillow Lace."

There are two sorts of toilé, one the usual woven texture, as of a piece of cambric, the other a more open arrangement of the threads, which is used for shading effects.

Relief is given to certain details of flowers and fibres of leaves by a flattened and slightly raised plaited cordonnet. A slight modelling is imparted to flowers by means of a bone instrument, which gives concave shapes to petals, leaves, and other ornaments.

There were two kinds of ground used in Brussels lace—the bride and the réseau. The bride was first employed, but was already discontinued in 1761, and was then only made to order.* Sometimes the bride and the réseau were combined.†

The ground used in Brussels lace is of two kinds—needlepoint and pillow. The needlepoint réseau is made in small segments of an inch in width, and from 7 to 45 inches long, joined together by a stitch long known as "fine joining," consisting of a fresh stitch formed with a needle between the two pieces to be united. The needleground is stronger, but three times more expensive than the pillow, which has a hexagonal mesh, of which two sides are made of four threads plaited four times, and four sides of two threads twisted twice. Since machine-made net has come into use, the vrai réseau is rarely made, save for royal orders. Of course, lace-makers so skilful as those of Brussels occasionally made experiments with other grounds, such as the star-meshed réseau ; but this is uncommon.

Brussels needlepoint was introduced into that city about 1720, evidently in imitation of the Alençon fabric, which it closely resembles in pattern and general effect. The Brussels needlepoint, however, is not so firm and precise, and the toilé is of looser make than the French work. The button-hole stitched cordonnet—a distinguishing feature of Alençon—is replaced by a single thread‡ or strand of threads. The Brussels needle-made réseau is made with a simple looped stitch.§

* "Dictionnaire du Citoyen," 1761.

† "Une coëffure à une piece d'Angleterre bride et réseau" (Comptes de Madame du Barry, Bib. Nat., MSS. F. Fr. 8157-8).

‡ In the needlepoint laces of Brussels the cordonnet is *generally* only a thread, but in some few cases it is covered with button-hole stitches, as in point d'Alençon.

§ "Le point d'aiguille de Bruxelles fait pour imiter le point d'Alençon est loin d'avoir sa solidité et son travail artistique. Pour imiter la brode qui donne tant de

The earliest Brussels needlepoints were grounded with this needle-made réseau, but much of the best needlepoint is grounded with the more familiar pillow-made "droschel." The Alençon "modes" are rendered with great accuracy. In this kind of mixed lace the cordonnet is usually a single moderately thick thread. In a specimen in the Dublin Museum, the cordonnet is like that of Alençon lace, buttonhole stitched, but the stitchery is not very close or regular.*

The making of Brussels lace is so complicated, wrote Mrs Palliser, that each process is assigned to different hands, who work only at her own special department, the first termed :—

1. Drocheleuse (Flemish, drocheles), makes the vrai réseau.

2. Dentelière (kantwerkes), the footing.

3. Pointeuse (needlewerkes), the point à l'aiguille flowers.

4. Platteuse (platwerkes), the plat flowers.

5. Fonneuse (groundwerkes) is charged with the open-work (jours) in the plat.

6. Jointeuse or attacheuse (lashwerkes) unites the different sections of the ground together.

7. Striqueuse or appliqueuse (strikes) is charged with the sewing (application) of the flowers upon the ground.†

The pattern is designed by the head of the fabric, who, having cut the parchment into pieces, hands it out ready pricked. The worker has no reflections to make, no combinations to study ; the whole responsibility rests with the master, who selects the ground, chooses the thread, and alone knows the effect to be produced as a whole. "The same design," writes Peuchet, "was never executed twice ; continual variations were introduced."‡

cachet au point d'Alençon et qui est fort longue à faire, on l'a remplacée dans le point d'aiguille de Bruxelles par un gros fil passé dans les mailles pour entourer le dessin" (Mme. Despierres, "Histoire du Point d'Alençon").

* No. 40, Dublin Museum.

† Mrs Palliser, "History of Lace," p. 122, edition 1902.

‡ "Le dessin est le premier objet de son attention ; il (le fabricant) le varie continuellement et ne fait exécuter le même une seconde fois . . . il en détache les fleurs en les piquant d'un millier d'épingles pour faciliter aux ouvrières la lecture du dessin, et les mettre à portée de l'exécuter avec exactitude. C'est lui qui juge des fonds les plus convenables pour faire ressortir les fleurs du dessin, pour donner à la dentelle l'éclat et la finesse."

The fineness of thread used in Brussels lace is almost a fable. " It is made of the flax grown in Brabant, at Hal and Rebecq-Rognon. The finest quality is spun in dark underground rooms, for contact with the dry air causes the thread to break, so fine is it as almost to escape the sight. The threadspinner closely examines every inch drawn from her distaff, and when any irregularity occurs, stops her wheel to repair the mischief. A background of dark paper is placed to throw out the thread, and the room so arranged as to admit one single ray of light upon the work." * †

Representation of objects naturalistically treated is one of the characteristics of Brussels work. In eighteenth-century specimens accurately rendered leaves and flowers,—in especial the pink and the tulip and the rose,—insects and birds are the main components of the design. ‡

In larger and more important pieces of the last years of the seventeenth and the beginning of the eighteenth centuries, the structure of the design is most elaborate, and figures, " subjects," and every variety of plant-form are most skilfully rendered. In a flounce given by Madame de Maintenon to François de Salignac de la Mothe Fénélon, who was consecrated Archbishop of Cambray in 1695, the ground is of brides picotées.§ In the two later specimens in the Musée des Arts Décoratifs in Brussels (one of which is dated 1720, while the other belongs to the early eighteenth century), a centre of the réseau ground contrasts with the surrounding border of brides picotées (Plates XLIX. and L.). The cravat-end in the possession of Miss Josephs is entirely grounded with the réseau (Plate LII.).

---

* Mrs Palliser, " History of Lace," edition 1902.

† Thread spun by machine in England from Belgian flax is much used now in Belgium. It has, however, never arrived at the fineness of that made by hand, and frequently in it there are traces of cotton, which depreciate its quality.

‡ " A Gênes, à Milan, à Venise, les dentelles au fuseau moins fines de matière se reconnaissent surtout aux détails de la composition. L'ornement y reste plus conventionnel et, lorsque les personnages et les animaux y apparaissent, ils sont d'expression allégorique. Le même genre de dentelle au fuseau fabriqué à Bruxelles ou en France contiendra des détails plus réalistes, les personnages y porteront le costume contemporain, les animaux y seront représentés sous la forme active " (" Le Musée Historique des Tissus de Lyon." R. Cox, Lyon, 1902).

§ Victoria and Albert Museum, No. 755, 1890.

Plate I.

PANEL OF BRUSSELS LACE.
Dated 1720.

Plate LI.

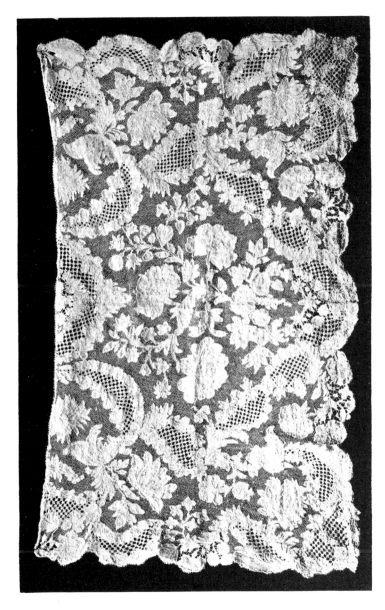

CRAVAT END OF BRUSSELS LACE.
Eighteenth century.

Plate LII.

CRAVAT END OF BRUSSELS LACE.

Eighteenth century. (*In the possession of Miss Josephs.*)

The two specimens from the Musée des Arts Décoratifs are very wonderful pieces of work. The dated piece (1720) represents the Invention of the Cross by Saint Helena, whose train is carried by an Eastern attendant. The second piece represents the pope seated under a canopy presenting or receiving a document from a lady who kneels before him. Her train is borne by an Eastern attendant, and her crown by a lady who stands behind her. The work upon the costumes is remarkable. Among the scroll work are angels blowing trumpets, and others beating drums.

During the reign of Louis XV. Brussels lace was much affected by the French court, and was almost preferred to point d'Alençon. This produced a certain French style of design in Brussels to meet this demand. In large designs figures, whimsical devices, and mottoes were introduced. Some of the details are graceful and ornamental; others, again, are misshapen. There is a distinct reflection of French mannerisms in Brussels of this period*—the balanced designs of repeated similar groups of fragmentary floral sprays, the valanced canopy, the royal attributes, cupids, pillars, trophies, &c., and the waved bands or ribbons dividing the design into compartments, and worked with very varied modes † (Plate LIII.).

In the last years of the seventeenth and in the early part of the eighteenth centuries, ornamentation in the Chinese style, fantastic zigzag forms, pagodas, and Indian or Chinese figures were introduced —a reflection of the taste that demanded negro attendants, and Oriental lacquer plaques inlaid on furniture. The Chinese influence may have received an impetus from that Siamese embassy which is said to have brought over many specimens of Chinese lacquer work as presents to Louis XIV.

Two specimens of the Louis XV. period belonging to Mme. Doistau and the Comtesse Foy, which were lent to the Exposition Internationale of 1900 at Paris, are good examples of this exotic style.

---

* And again at a later date, when a number of lace makers left France for Belgium after the French Revolution. To-day the influence of French design is as strong as ever.

† Brussels pillow-renderings of various modes, used in French needlepoint, the Argentan hexagonal mesh, the réseau rosacé, star-devices, &c., are very close and skilful.

K

Mme. Doistau's piece (which is bobbin lace) is a square cravat end, showing motifs of pagodas, and the longtailed crested bird that so often accompanies them. The point lace belonging to the Comtesse Foy shows the influence of the design of Dresden china in the little kiosks, the minute landscapes, rocks and rivers, among which are huntsmen and dogs chasing stags.

Brussels in the late eighteenth century followed French laces in the change that took place on the accession of Louis XVI., when design became "thinner," and the lace appeared to be mostly réseau, edged with a stiff rectilinear border of conventional design, the ground powdered with little detached flowers, sprays, and, later, spots and rosettes.

In the early nineteenth century the pseudo-classic style of ornament then in vogue in France influenced Brussels design. The introduction of machine-made net, upon which Brussels bobbin-made flowers were applied (Brussels appliqué), also had an influence upon design.

In France the term point d'Angleterre is used for Brussels lace. This is somewhat confusing, as point d'Angleterre was a term applied in the late seventeenth century to a variety of Flemish pillow lace, of which the design was in imitation of the scroll patterns of point lace of that date. Flanders lace was worn almost exclusively during the reign of Charles I. and the Commonwealth, and in 1662 an Act was passed by the English Parliament, alarmed at the sums of money expended on foreign goods, prohibiting the importation of all foreign lace. The English lace dealers endeavoured to improve the national fabric by inviting Flemish lace makers to settle in England, and establish a manufacture there,* but when this scheme proved abortive they adopted the simpler experiment of smuggling in Brussels lace, and selling it under the name of Point d'Angleterre —a term which, like point d'Espagne and "flat Spanish," relates to the country that consumed it rather than that which produced it.

This fact is corroborated in a memorandum by the Venetian

---

* Peuchet gives a somewhat different account. "Les fabricans Anglais, pour favoriser les premiers essais de leurs manufactures, achetaient beaucoup de dentelles de Bruxelles qu'ils vendaient à toute l'Europe sous le nom de point d'Angleterre " (" Dictionnaire Universel de la Géographie Commerçante," 1799).

Plate LIII.

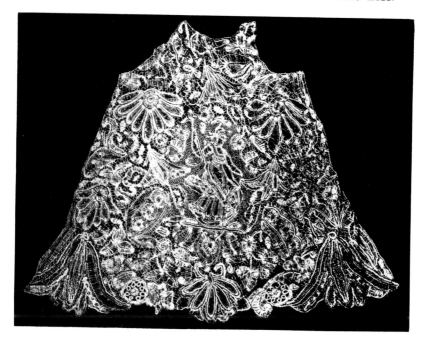

FRAGMENT OF BRUSSELS LACE.
Beginning of eighteenth century.

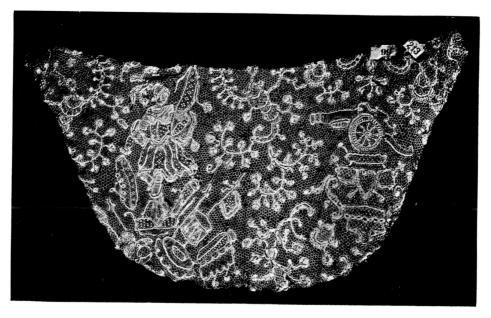

FRAGMENT OF BRUSSELS LACE.
Showing French influence in the design.   Early eighteenth century.

Plate LIV.

BORDER OF BRUSSELS LACE.
Early eighteenth century.

BORDER OF BRUSSELS LACE.
Eighteenth century.

ambassador to the English court in 1695, who states that Venetian point is no longer in fashion, but " that called English point, which, you know, is not made here, but in Flanders, and only bears the name of English to distinguish it from the others."* The name point d'Angleterre is used nowadays, of a variety of Brussels lace, with many open fillings of the bride variety.

* Quoted in Mrs Palliser's " History of Lace," edition 1902, p. 117.

CHAPTER X.

MECHLIN AND ANTWERP LACE.

PRIOR to 1665 nearly all Flanders laces were known under the name of Mechlin to the French commercial world. "The common people here," writes Regnard, who visited Flanders in 1681, "as throughout all Flanders, occupy themselves in making the white lace known as Malines." The laces of Ypres, Bruges, Dunkirk, and Courtrai, according to Savary, passed under the name of Mechlin at Paris. Peuchet writes that a great deal of Malines was made in Antwerp,* Mechlin, and Brussels, and that the industry was an important one at Antwerp. He adds that an excellent quality of thread is made in the town and neighbourhood.

In England Mechlin is not mentioned by name until Queen Anne's reign.†

In 1699 the Act prohibiting foreign lace was repealed in so far as it touched the Spanish Low Countries, and Anne, while prohibiting lace made "in the dominions of the French King," admits the import of Flanders lace, so that from the first years of the eighteenth century Mechlin was without rival in England among light laces. According to Peuchet, Mechlin laces are "les plus belles, après celles de Bruxelles, et elles ont un peu plus de durée." It was eminently suited to the less severe modern costume which came in with the eighteenth century, and by reason of its open à jours and transparent appearance was worn

---

* Specimens of Mechlin lace are preserved in the Steen Museum at Antwerp.

† "Flanders lace" is the only term used for Flemish laces in the Great Wardrobe Accounts until Queen Anne, when "Macklin" and Brussels are first noted down.

Plate LV.

PART OF A LAPPET OF MECHLIN LACE.

Showing quatrefoil filling. Eighteenth century.

BORDER OF MECHLIN LACE.

Dated 1757.

Plate LVI.

BORDER OF MECHLIN LACE.
With medallions of scriptural subjects.

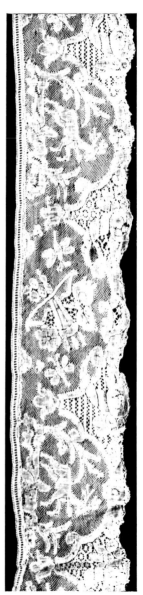

BORDERS OF MECHLIN LACE.
Eighteenth century.

as a trimming lace. It thus remained in fashion through the eighteenth century, when references like " Mechlin the queen of lace,"* " Mechlin the finest lace of all,"† bear witness to a vogue in England little short of extraordinary. The disappearance of lace ruffles before 1780 from women's sleeves, and the disappearance of the cravat and men's ruffles, put an end to lace as a fashionable adjunct to dress. In 1834 there were but eight houses where it was fabricated.‡ Unfortunately, also, for the prosperity of the industry, Mechlin is of all laces the easiest to copy in machine-made lace.

Historically, Mechlin developed, like Valenciennes, from the straight-edged laces of indefinite pattern, with an irregular ground§ which has the appearance of being pierced at intervals with round holes. ‖

The earliest examples of what we can recognise as Mechlin show a design consisting of groupings of heavily drawn flowers, clumsily designed rococo devices, cornucopias, &c.

Later, with the adoption of the characteristic Mechlin réseau, the floral design becomes more delicate and light, and a French influence is apparent (Plate LVII.). Much of this lace, worn in France during the Regency and later, was made up in the style of modern insertion, with an edging on both sides,¶ campané or scalloped, and used for the gathered trimmings called "quilles," like the Argentan sleeve-trimmings of Madame Louise de France, painted by Nattier in 1748.

The attempt to imitate Alençon extended not only to the motifs

---

* Young, " Love of Fame."

† Anderson, " Origin of Commerce."

‡ Mechlin lace was also made at Antwerp, Lierre, and Turnhout. " There was a fine collection of Mechlin lace in the Paris Exhibition of 1867 from Turnhout, and some other localities " (Mrs Palliser, " History of Lace ").

§ See Chapter on Valenciennes.

‖ In the Gruuthus collection, laces of this type which have " points d'esprit " (small solid portions like the millet seed of Genoese lace) are invariably attributed to Mechlin, while in the Musée des Arts Décoratifs at Brussels they are attributed to Antwerp.

¶ 1741. " Une coiffure de nuit de Malines à raizeau campanée de deux pieces " (" Inv. de Mademoiselle de Clermont ").

1761. "Une paire de manches de Malines bridée non campanée" (" Inv. de la Duchesse de Modène ").

of its design—the characteristic winding ribbon and scattered sprays
of flowers,* but to the buttonhole-stitched cordonnet. In Mechlin a
coarse thread was applied to the edges of the design, which gives
higher relief than the flat cordonnet.† The fillings are often, like
Alençon, of the trellis type.

The late eighteenth-century Mechlin has pieces quite undis-
tinguishable in design from Alençon of the Louis XVI. period, no
doubt owing to its large consumption in France, as a "summer lace."
The very characteristic pattern of a flower (sun-flower?) in full
blossom, and with closing petals, is often met with in Mechlin laces
of the end of the eighteenth century. This lace has a border with a
very shallow scallop or slightly waved. The pattern of repeated
sprigs of flowers, or of leaves, follows the edge. The remaining
ground is covered with small square spots, minute quatrefoils, or
leaflets. The flower is Flemish in treatment,‡ while the semés upon
the réseau show the French influence of the late eighteenth century
(Plate LVIII.).

Design in Mechlin is in general floral in character. But a curious
figured design is illustrated in Séguin's "La Dentelle" (plate xiv.,
fig. 1), and characterised by him as "une niaserie enfantine." This
piece, which dates from the last years of Louis XV., represents two
men in a carriage driving a horse. The men wear three-cornered
hats, long coats, ruffles ; two birds are flying in the air, and the group
is separated from its repeat by an ill-drawn tree. A piece in the
Victoria and Albert Museum,§ has a pattern of trees, buds, and scrolls,
with cupids blowing horns and shooting at winged and burning hearts.
A fragment of an altar cloth in the Gruuthus Museum ‖ shows a
medallion containing figures representing some scriptural scene. A
similar piece, including several similar medallions, is in the Musée des
Arts Décoratifs at Brussels (Plate LVI.).

---

* The sprigs in Mechlin are, however, clumsier in drawing.

† No. 1297, 1872, in the Victoria and Albert Museum shows this thick twisted
thread stitched to the gimp of the flower or pattern.

‡ Some of the designs of Mechlin show very careful naturalistic presentment
of flowers.

§ No. 1400, 1874.

‖ Litt. B., No. 6.

Plate LVII.

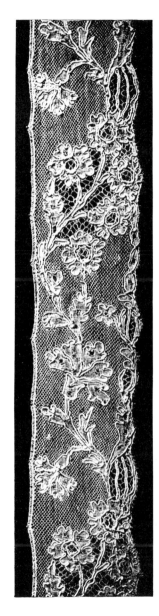

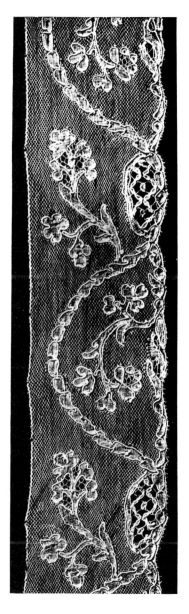

BORDERS OF MECHLIN.

Showing Alençon influence in its design, and in the coarse cordonnet.

Plate LVIII.

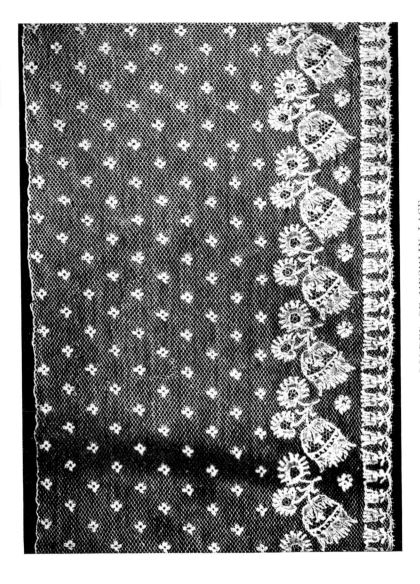

BORDER OF MECHLIN LACE.

Late eighteenth century.

The ground and ornament of Mechlin, like Valenciennes, are made in one piece on the pillow, and many and various experimental fancy groundings were tried before adopting the hexagon-meshed réseau made of two threads twisted twice on four sides, and four threads plaited three times on the two other sides—producing a shorter plait and a smaller mesh than that of the Brussels réseau.

The early grounds are varieties of the "fond de neige," and the fond-chant or six-pointed star mesh is met with. A réseau of interlaced double threads is also of frequent occurrence, and a réseau of four threads plaited to form a very large mesh having the effect of an enlarged fond-chant ground.

The most common form of ornamental filling is an arrangement of linked quatrefoils.

The toilé is finer and less close in texture than Valenciennes, and appears to be now dense and cloudy, now thin and almost transparent. This unevenness of quality, together with the presence of the cordonnet (which gives precision to the ornament), is responsible for the old name of 'broderie de Malines." *

ANTWERP LACE.

Antwerp, though an old lace-making centre (p. 50), is remarkable for only one type of peasant lace, the "potten kant," so called from the representation of a pot of flowers with which it is almost always decorated. Mrs Palliser considered the motif to be a survival from an earlier design, including the figure of the Virgin and the Annunciation, though it does not appear that any such composition has been met with.† The motif of a vase of flowers, however, is a

* " Une paire de manchettes de dentelle de Malines brodée" (Inv. de decès de Mademoiselle de Charollais, 1758).

† "The flower-pot was a symbol of the Annunciation. In the early representations of the appearance of the Angel Gabriel to the Virgin Mary, lilies are placed either in his hand, or set as an accessory in a vase. As Romanism declined, the angel disappeared, and the lily-pot became a vase of flowers ; subsequently the Virgin was omitted, and there only remained the vase of flowers" (Mrs Palliser).

common one among Flemish and Belgian laces; and the flowers are not restricted to the Annunciation lilies—roses, pinks, sunflowers, and other flowers being met with.

The ground varies from a coarse fond-chant *—a six-pointed star réseau, or, as it is better described, a diamond crossed by two horizontal threads—to various large meshed coarse and fancy grounds. The laces are usually straight-edged. The pot, or vase, or basket is not always part of the design; a stiff group of flowers, throwing out branches to right and left, is almost invariable. Sometimes pendant festoons or garlands, or bunches of flowers are met with.† The cordonnet of strong untwisted thread often appears too coarse for the toilé, and outlines it with short loops. Antwerp lace appears in a portrait of Anna Goos (1627 to 1691) in the Plantin Museum at Antwerp. The date of the portrait is between 1665-70, and the lace, which is straight-edged, has a thin scroll pattern upon a réseau ground.

* The name chant is an abbreviation of Chantilly, in which lace the fond-chant réseau is much used.

† No. 1570, 1872, Victoria and Albert Museum, is a border of Antwerp lace with a loosely twisted sort of *œil de perdrix* ground, and pattern of flowers and leaves. The outline to the pattern and the gimp of the leaves and flowers are like those seen in some of the early eighteenth-century Mechlin laces.

Plate LIX.

BORDER OF ANTWERP "POTTEN KANT."

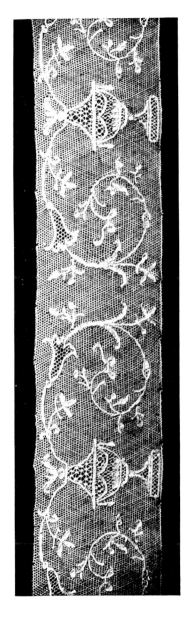

BORDER OF ANTWERP "POTTEN KANT."
With "fond chant" ground.

CHAPTER XI.

VALENCIENNES AND DUTCH LACE.

VALENCIENNES, part of the ancient province of Hainault, together with Lille and Arras, is French by conquest and treaty.* The lace fabric was introduced there from Le Quesnoy, one of the towns mentioned in the ordinance of 5th August 1665, which founded on a large scale the manufacture of point de France. Some years before, in 1646, a certain Mlle. Françoise Badar † had brought from Antwerp some young girls, whom she intended to teach lace-making, and for this purpose she took a house in the Rue de Tournay (now Rue de Lille). She afterwards undertook the direction of several manufactures, among them that of Le Quesnoy, which she left in a prosperous condition on her death in 1677, the date that the town of Valenciennes was taken by Louis XIV.

The lace of Le Quesnoy is never mentioned after Louis XIV., and after that reign Valenciennes comes into notice, but there is no record of the transfer of the fabric. The fond de neige ‡ is supposed to be a tradition derived from the workwomen of Le Quesnoy. Valenciennes, from its position as a commercial centre, was well fitted to carry on

---

* French Hainault, French Flanders, and Cambrésis (the present Dép. du Nord), with Artois, were conquests of Louis XIII. and Louis XIV., confirmed to France by the treaties of Aix-la-Chapelle (1668) and Nimeguen (1678). In 1656 the Spaniards under Condé made a successful defence against the French under Turenne, but in 1677 Louis XIV. took the town, and it has always since belonged to France.

† "Vie de Mlle. Françoise Badar," Liège, 1726.

‡ "Les directrices du bureau du Quesnoy avaient, en effet, adopté un genre special ce fond de neige qu'elles enseignerènt aux ouvrières Valenciennoises" (A. Carlier, "Les Valenciennes").

the industry, and the fact that the town had its "brodeurs" and "passementiers"* aided in its development. It reached its climax from 1725 to 1780, when there were from 3,000 to 4,000 lace-makers in the city alone, and the art was largely practised in the country round, to judge by the quantity of fausse Valenciennes.†

Existing specimens of the Louis XIV. period—for we have not the evidence of portraits as a corroboration, as Valenciennes was never a "dentelle de grande toilette"—appear closely to resemble the designs of Venice à réseau. In specimens Nos. 416, 1872, and 913, 1901, of the Victoria and Albert Museum, the long rolling scroll throwing out a number of small cut-up leaves, the large ornamental fruit—like a conventionalised pomegranate with leafy crest—are among the motifs of the fine type of late Venetian à réseau, but the Italian lace, with its clear and even needle réseau, contrasts favourably with the confused "neigeux" Valenciennes pillow ground of minute solid circles, sometimes surrounded by other circles.

Valenciennes was used in negligés, the trimmings of sheets, pillow-cases, nightgowns, nightcaps, for ruffles, for barbes, fichus, and "tours de gorge." In the "Etat d'un Trousseau," 1771, among the necessary articles are enumerated, "Une coeffure, tour de gorge et le fichu plissé de vraie Valenciennes"; and Madame du Barry had lappets and pillow-cases trimmed with Valenciennes. It was not used as a Church lace, being fine and ineffective.

From 1780 downwards there was less demand for a lace of the quality of Valenciennes, and with the Revolution this, with more than thirty French fabrics, disappeared. In a manuscript of M. Tordois's "coup d'œil sur Valenciennes" (de l'an IX. à l'an XIII.), we read that in the year IX. there was a cessation in the production of lace-thread. Three ateliers were subsequently established, but this

---

* "L'industrie des brodeurs et des passementiers, qui était pratiquée dans cette ville à la même époque, contribue à l'épanouissement de la dentelle. Tel fut d'ailleurs la raison de l'article 21 de l'édit de l'an 1653, conférant aux maîtres passementiers le privilège exclusif de la fabrication des passements aux fuseaux, aux épingles, et sur l'oreiller" (A. Carlier, "Les Valenciennes").

† In the seventeenth century "L'hôpital de Lille renfermait sept cent ouvrières faisant de la fausse valenciennes, très rapprochante de la vraie ; on comptait tant dans cette ville que dans les environs quinze mille ouvrières travaillant de la dentelle bâtarde du fond Paris, et du fond clair" (A. Carlier, "Les Valenciennes").

Plate LX.

BORDER OF EARLY VALENCIENNES. Late seventeenth or early eighteenth century.

With neigeux ground.

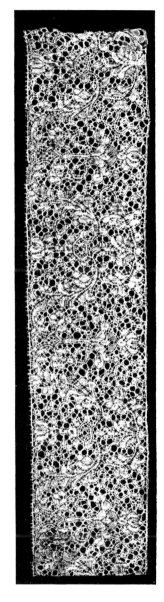

BORDER OF EARLY VALENCIENNES. Late seventeenth century.

With neigeux ground and confused design.

Plate LXI.

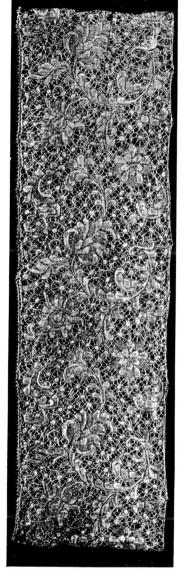

BORDER OR INSERTION OF EARLY VALENCIENNES.

Late seventeenth or early eighteenth century.

BORDER OR INSERTION OF EARLY VALENCIENNES

Late seventeenth or early eighteenth century.

short artistic revival had no permanent result; in 1800 there were only a few hundred lace-workers within the walls; and in 1851, in spite of the efforts of Napoleon III. to revive the industry, there were only two lace-workers remaining, both upwards of eighty years of age.

Narrow straight-edged borders of pillow lace were probably made in Valenciennes and in French Flanders in the early seventeenth century consisting of running closely crowded and indefinite designs, with a ground of a series of irregular or rounded holes between short brides; but extant pieces of Valenciennes belong mainly to the reigns of Louis XV. and XVI.

In the Louis XV. period and the late eighteenth century, the Flemish character of Valenciennes re-asserts itself in its choice of motifs such as tulips, carnations, and anemones, naturalistically treated and occasionally heavy in outline; the characteristic clear réseau ground in the subsequent reign occupies much of the place originally destined for the design, but towards 1780 little lace was made, and the disappearance of ruffles from the masculine costume added greatly to the depression. Among Empire pieces is a curious specimen once in the possession of M. Dupont Auberville, representing Napoleon I. as an equestrian Cæsar facing the Empress Josephine; while the Imperial arms, flanked at the base by cannons and flags, appear between the two.

In Valenciennes, unlike Brussels and Milanese pillow lace, the ground is worked at the same time as the pattern, that is to say, threads are brought out from the pattern to form the réseau and carried back into the pattern, so that the threads do not follow the lines of the ornament, as they do in all pillow laces where the ornament or toilé is made separately. The Valenciennes method thus requires an enormous number of pins, because each thread must be kept in place until the whole width of the pattern is worked.

Like Mechlin, the ground went through various modifications—including the fond de neige already noticed as accompanying early scroll patterns—before the réseau was finally fixed. Several of these ornamental grounds are used in various portions of the design, in the edging in Plate LXII., where two or three varieties can be counted, which are much thicker and closer in effect than the characteristic Valenciennes réseau. In this ground each side of its mesh, which is more diamond than hexagon in shape, is formed of four threads plaited together. The clearly marked hexagonal mesh of the Mechlin réseau is also formed of four threads, but only two of its sides are plaited, the other four being twisted.

Fancy grounds (Plate LXII.) were produced side by side with the above-described mesh, as the accounts of Madame du Barry bear witness, until late in the eighteenth century. When their grounds were thus mixed and varied, such laces, although their patterns are almost identically the same as those of Valenciennes with the pure réseau, are termed "fausses Valenciennes." This has been taken to mean that these laces were made in the neighbourhood of the town of Valenciennes, in Hainault, and elsewhere, not in Valenciennes itself, where the simple distinctive réseau alone was used.

A legend has arisen about vraie ' Valenciennes." In support of the theory that the "true" lace was only made in the town itself, M. Dieudonné, Préfet du Nord in 1804, wrote : "This beautiful manu-facture is so inherent in the place that it is an established fact that if a piece of lace were begun at Valenciennes and finished outside the walls, the part which had not been made at Valenciennes would be visibly less beautiful and less perfect than the other, though continued by the same lace-maker with the same thread on the same pillow." M. Dieudonné attributed it to the influence of the atmosphere.

" All by the same hand " we find entered in the bills of the lace-sellers of the time. The superiority of the city-made lace no doubt depended largely on the fact that it was made in underground cellars, in which the dampness* of the air affected the "tension " of the very fine thread in use. In a drier atmosphere outside the walls, a different result would be obtained, even by the same workwoman, with the same cushion and thread, though it is doubtful whether the experiment has ever been actually tried.† The necessity for a humid atmosphere was recognised early in the eighteenth century. In an

---

* "En 1780 plusieurs milliers de dentellières travaillaient dans l'enceinte de la ville, généralement dans des caves ou des chambres basses. Grâce à l'humidité le fil était de retors, ou ne se détordait pas, et conservait toute sa force " (A. Carlier, " Les Valenciennes ").

† " Le fil employé pour quelques pièces fines était d'une telle susceptibilité que l'haleine de l'ouvrière le modifiait et que sa teinte se trouvait influencée par le soleil et l'humidité " (A. Carlier, " Les Valenciennes ").

Plate LXII.

PORTION OF A LAPPET OF VALENCIENNES.
Wire ground.

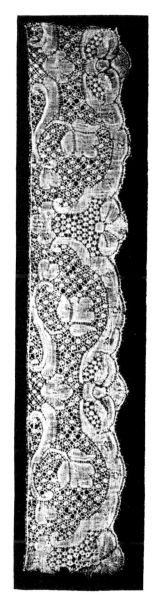

EDGING OF VALENCIENNES.
Showing various fancy grounds.   Early eighteenth century.

extract from the " Procès Verbaux du Bureau du Commerce," 1727, it is stated that in Holland or in England it would be impossible to "conserver les filets dans le point de fraicheur et d'humidité convenables pour façonner des toillettes." *

According to Peuchet the sole defect of Valenciennes was its indifferent white; only one quality of thread was used, the value of which in Arthur Young's time ranged from 24 to 700 livres a pound, but though expensive, the price of the flax was but one-thirtieth of the selling price of the finished lace. This thread came from Flanders, Hainault, and Cambrésis.

The designs were pricked upon green parchment prepared at Lille, and a favourite pattern remained in use as long as it was in demand.

The design was the special property of the manufacturer, and it was at the option of the worker to pay for its use and retain her work, if not satisfied with the price she received. Valenciennes can be detected no matter what its design, which is often derivative, imitative, or directly borrowed from Mechlin, Brussels, or Alençon, by the absence of cordonnet and by its peculiar mesh. Some rare experimental specimens were made by the Valenciennes workers in which an occasional cordonnet was introduced, but such works are very exceptional. Open à jours are of extremely rare occurrence; their fillings are very similar to those of Mechlin.

No lace was so expensive to make, the reason being the number of bobbins required for fine lace of wide width. "While Lille lace-workers could produce from three to five ells a day, those of Valenciennes could not complete more than an inch and a half in the same time. It took ten months, working fifteen hours a day, to finish a pair of men's ruffles, hence the costliness of the lace." † At the present day in the Valenciennes lace made in Brabant all the bobbins which are employed in the "mats" or ornament do not pass into the ground, which is a great economy; they are removed to the next motif.

After the French Revolution, when so many lace-makers fled to

---

* Quoted in Mme. Laurence de Laprade, "Le Poinct de France," 1904.
† Mrs Palliser, "History of Lace."

M

Belgium—Ghent, Alost, Ypres,* Bruges, Menin, and Courtrai† became the centres of a new and inferior Valenciennes, each town having a distinctive feature in the ground. These laces are as a rule less close in workmanship, less solid, and cheaper.

At Ypres, which makes the best quality of Belgian Valenciennes, the réseau is made of a plait of four threads, and forms a diamond-shaped mesh. In Courtrai and Menin the grounds are twisted three and a half times; and in Bruges, where the ground has a circular mesh, the bobbins are twisted three times; that made at Ghent,‡ in East Flanders, is square-meshed, the bobbins being twisted two and a half times. Valenciennes laces made outside the walls of Valenciennes were designated as fausses Valenciennes, whether made in Belgium or in the Départment du Nord, at Lille, Bergues, Bailleul, Avesnes, Cassel, and Armentières. § Of these latter centres Bailleul‖ produced the largest quantity: chiefly (before 1830) of a narrow straight-edged type for the Normandy market.

At Dieppe, in Normandy, Valenciennes with the square ground was introduced in 1826, by the sisters Fleury and Hubert from the Convent of La Providence at Rouen, and took the place of the old point de Dieppe, which is very like Valenciennes with small round meshes. Of this lace Peuchet says that the designs were inferior, but that an attempt was being made to introduce lighter, less crowded designs. The thread came from Flanders, from Saint Amant. Point

---

* As early as 1656 Ypres began to make lace. In 1684 it was already much decayed. It rose again after the influx of Valenciennes workmen after the French Revolution. In 1833 the wire ground was adopted.

† "Courtrai makes the widest Valenciennes. Valenciennes of Courtrai was much sought after in the eighteenth century both in England and France" (Peuchet).

‡ Savary cites the fausses Valenciennes of Ghent, which he declares are "moins serrées, un peu moins solides, et un peu moins chères."

§ "Armentières et Bailleul ne font que de la Valenciennes fausse dans tous les prix" (Peuchet).

‖ The laces of Bailleul "have neither the finish nor the lightness of the Belgian products, are soft to touch, the mesh round, and the ground thick, but it is strong and cheap, and in general use for trimming lace" (Mrs Palliser, "History of Lace").

Plate LXIII.

BORDER OF DUTCH LACE.
Early seventeenth century.

Plate LXIV.

BORDER OF DUTCH LACE.
Late seventeenth or eighteenth century.

Plate LXV.

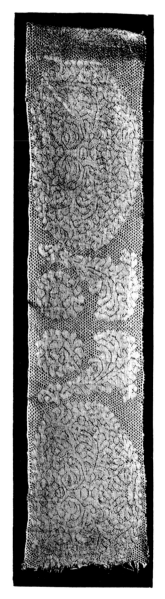

BORDER OR INSERTION OF DUTCH LACE.
Late seventeenth century.

EDGING OR INSERTION OF DUTCH LACE.
Valenciennes type.

de Dieppe requires much fewer bobbins, and whereas Valenciennes can only be made in lengths of eight inches without detaching the lace from the pillow, the Dieppe point is not taken off, but rolled.

DUTCH LACE.

Holland, in spite of its proximity to Flanders, seems to have produced little lace during the sixteenth and early seventeenth centuries. In 1667, however, the Dutch themselves set up manufactures of lace, to rival France, which had laid prohibitive duties upon foreign goods.

No trace is found of the manufacture of point lace set up at Amsterdam by refugees from Alençon. The Dutch lace, as it appears in portraits, is thick, strong, and bobbin made. A type of scalloped lace, the pattern of each scallop repeating upon either side of a central line, has a design of tape like continuous scrolls arranged rather closely together in leafy or fan forms, or some pendant blossom of conventional form ; * this lace was in use from about 1630 to 1650. † Other Dutch varieties of lace are pieces in design like early Valenciennes with conventional rolling scroll with blossoms ; or a pattern of flowers and fruit strictly copied from nature. The ground is generally of small irregular meshes.

The thread used in Holland was the famous Haarlem thread, once considered the best adapted for lace-makers in the world. " No place bleaches flax like the meer of Haarlem."

---

* Among the Dutch laces in the Victoria and Albert Museum is a pillow-made edging in the manner of early Italian pillow-laces, but of thicker design (No. 604, 1854).

† See in the Victoria and Albert Museum, No. 286, 1890 ; No. 861, 1853 ; No. 153, 1885.

CHAPTER XII.

ALENÇON AND ARGENTAN.

A VERY full and accurate account of Alençon lace has been given by Madame Despierres* in her " Histoire du Point d'Alençon," and the revival of interest in the national lace industry, noticeable latterly in France, is responsible for a new work on the subject, " Le Poinct de France," of Madame Laurence de Laprade, which reproduces at length many interesting documents. The history of no other lace centre has been so exhaustively treated ; and any one interested in the historical side of the subject will find all available material in these two histories. The present account is concerned only with the development of the design of Alençon, and the process of its manufacture.

Colbert's attention was directed to the immense amount of money that was sent out of the kingdom ; nor must his personal inclinations and tastes be overlooked.†

Alençon, in Normandy, was chosen as one of the seats of the new manufacture, because the lace industry was already widespread among the peasants. Point coupé had been made there at an early date, possibly introduced by Catherine de Medicis, to whom Charles IX.

---

* Mme. G. Despierres, " Histoire du Point d'Alençon," 1886.

† " Dès 1650 Colbert s'initia, lui aussi, à la culture de ces beaux-arts qu'il devait un jour protéger avec tant d'efficacité. Envoyé par Mazarin à Rome, à Florence, à Gênes, à Turin, s'il échoua parfois dans les missions diplomatiques . . . du moins ne négligea-t-il aucune occasion d'accroître les richesses artistiques de celui dont il représentait et les goûts fastueux et la politique astucieuse " (" Les Manufactures Nationales ").

Plate LXVI.

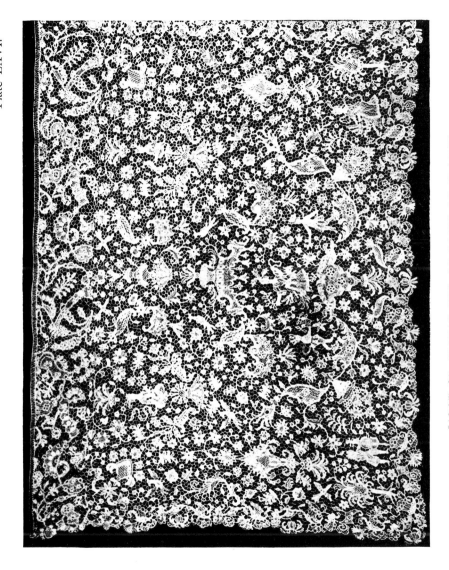

JABOT OR CRAVAT END OF POINT DE FRANCE.

With a design of a pseudo-Oriental character.   End of seventeenth century.

PORTION OF A WIDE
Ei

Plate LXVII.

OF POINT DE FRANCE.
y.

Plate LXVIII.

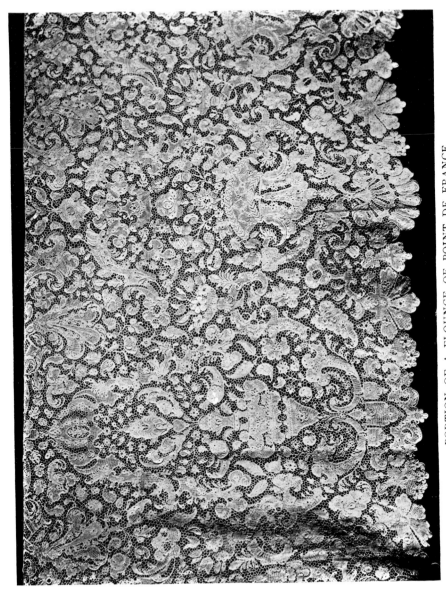

PORTION OF A FLOUNCE OF POINT DE FRANCE.

Eighteenth century. (*In the possession of Mrs Christie Miller.*)

had given the Duchy of Alençon. About 1650, according to Madame Despierres, it appears from a letter of Favier-Duboulay, intendant of Alençon, that points de Venise were successfully imitated and introduced into Alençon by "une femme nommée La Perriere, fort habile à ces ouvrages,"* thus causing the gradual disappearance of point coupé. More than eight thousand persons were employed in lace-making in Alençon, Séez, Argentan, Falaise, and in the neighbouring parishes.

It is no doubt to this long apprenticeship in lace-making that the supremacy of Alençon among French laces is due. An ordinance of 15th August 1665 founded the manufacture of points de France, with an exclusive privilege for ten years ; a company was formed, and the manufacture realised enormous profits until 1675, when the monopoly expired and was not renewed. The new manufactures had the advantage of high-handed protection on the part of the Government. On 17th November 1667 appears a fresh prohibition of the selling or wearing of passements, lace, and other works in thread of Venice, Genoa, and other foreign countries ; and on 17th March 1668 *itératives* —prohibitions—to wear these, as injurious to a manufacture of point which gives subsistence to a number of persons in this kingdom. In 1670 an Englishman travelling in France notices the efforts of the French Government to protect the points de France. "They are so set (he writes) in this country upon maintaining their own manufactures, that only two days ago there was publicly burnt by the hangman a hundred thousand crowns worth of point de Venise, Flanders lace, and other foreign commodities that are forbid." † Later, in 1680, it is stated in "Britannia Languens" that the laces commonly called points de Venise now come mostly from France, and amount to a vast sum yearly. In 1687, again, the fourth Earl of Manchester writes from Venice of the excessive dearness of the point made there, but is confident, either in Paris or England, "one may have it as cheap, and better patterns."

It is certain that the Italian style continued in vogue for the ten

* Letter from Favier-Duboulay, 7th September 1665. "Correspondence Administrative sous le Règne de Louis XIV.," vol. 3.

† R. Montagu to Lord Arlington. "MSS. of the Duke of Buccleuch," vol. i. Hist. MSS. Comm.

years of the monopoly (1665-75). There were Venetian workwomen to the number of twenty at Alençon in October 1665,[*] and in the same month a letter to Colbert is sanguine enough to hope to produce in a short time from the royal manufacture "des échantillons qui ne céderont en rien au véritable Venise." In 1673 these hopes are apparently justified, and Colbert is able to write to the Comte d'Avaux, who has sent him a point collar in high relief, that the French points can bear comparison with the products of Venice.[†]

The *Mercure*, which gives detailed chronicles of the new points de France, describes them in 1677 as having a floral design, brides à picots, and with "little flowers over the large, which might be styled flying flowers, being only attached in the centre,"—the fine raised work of flying loops, upon delicate rose points. The design, again, is exactly that characteristic of Venetian scroll patterns. "The flowers," the *Mercure* writes in 1678, "which are in higher relief in the centre, and lower at the edge, are united by small stalks and flowers."

The development of the new points was watched by Colbert, who writes, in 1682, that their principal defect is that they are not so firm or so white as the rival points of Venice.[‡]

Before the expiration of the privilege, the artists who furnished designs for all works undertaken for the Court of Louis XIV., must have supplied patterns for the royal manufacture. In the account of the King's buildings is the entry of a payment due to Bonnemer and to Bailly, the painter,[§] for several days' work with other painters in making designs for embroideries and points d'Espagne. These

---

* Lettre à Colbert, tome 132, fo. 75 ("Bibliothèque Nationale").

† "En Janvier, 1673, M. le Comte d'Avaux ayant remplacé Mgr. de Bonzy comme ambassadeur à Venise, Colbert lui écrit : " J'ai bien reçu le collet de point rebrodé en relief, que vous m'avez envoyé, et que j'ai trouvé fort beau. Je le confronterai avec ceux qui se font dans nos manufactures, mais je dois vous dire à l'avance que l'on en fait dans la royaume d'aussi beaux" (Lefébure, " Broderie et Dentelles ").

‡ A letter written, 2nd January 1682, by Colbert to M. de Montargis, Intendant at Alençon.

§ "Colbert chargea les plus grands artistes du temps, Le Brun, Bérain, Bailly, Bonnemer, de créer des modèles" (Mme. Laurence de Laprade, "Le Poinct de France ").

Plate LXIX.

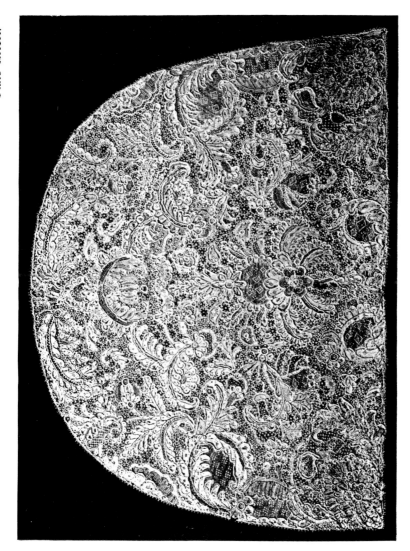

CAP CROWN OF ALENÇON.
With fancy grounds, eighteenth century.

N

Plate LXX.

SLEEVE TRIMMING OF ALENÇON.
Louis XV., first half of eighteenth century.

With ground of irregular hexagons.

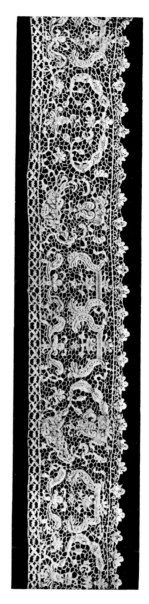

BORDER OF POINT DE FRANCE.
The pattern is made up of repeated groups of poorly-shaped devices on broken scrolls.
French, late seventeenth century.

Plate LXXI.

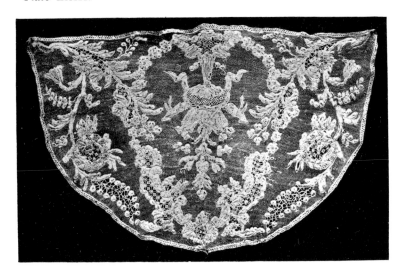

CAP CROWN OF ALENÇON.
With réseau ground.   Louis XIV., early eighteenth century.

ALENÇON.
With ground of hexagonal brides.   Louis XIV., late seventeenth century.

designs were jealously protected. None had permission to make the fine point of the royal pattern, except those who worked for the manufactory, and all girls had to show to the authorities the patterns they intended working, "so that the King shall be satisfied, and the people gain a livelihood."* That brides with picots, as well as brides claires, were made in the royal fabric, is mentioned in the *Mercure* of July 1673.†

After the expiration of the privilege (1675) the "fabricants" had designs specially made for them, which became their exclusive property. In 1680 they asked and obtained permission to prosecute certain small manufacturers who copied their patterns,‡ and in 1691 they speak of the "licence" of several manufacturers, who copy the designs of others instead of using "tout leur esprit et tout leur industrie à inventer de nouveaux dessins et des modèles plus parfaits et plus delicats."§

It was in 1675 that the name of point de France began to be confined to point d'Alençon, no doubt as the most important of the French fabrics.‖ Point d'Alençon is worked with a very fine needle, upon a parchment pattern. The parchment was originally used in its natural colour, but before 1769 green parchment had been adopted, as it is mentioned in an inventory of that date.¶ The

---

* Mrs Palliser, "History of Lace," edition 1902, p. 190.

† "On fait . . . des dentelles d'Espagne avec des brides claires sans picots ; et l'on fait aux nouveaux points de France des brides qui en sont remplies d'un nombre infini."

‡ "Gabriel Gence, Charles Guitton, et Louis Marescot, marchands trafiquant des ouvrages de vélin et point de France . . . vous remontrent que depuis trois ou quatre ans ils ont été obligez de faire de nouveaux dessings . . . lesquels reviennent à grand prix aux supplyants. Cependent quantité de personnes malveillantes dérobent les dits dessins. . . . Toutes lesquelles choses méritent un chastiment exemplaire, à l'encontre de ceux qui se trouvent coupables et dont il est presque impossible d'avoir révélation, si ce n'est par censures écclésiastiques " (" Archives de la Préfecture de L'Orne ").

§ Mme. Laurence de Laprade, "Le Poinct de France."

‖ "Après la dissolution de cette société (1675) le nom de point de France fut donné au point d'Alençon. Ce nom était aussi souvent usité dans les actes que ceux de vélin et de point d'Alençon, et ces trois noms ont été employés concurremment jusqu'à nos jours" ("Histoire du Point d'Alençon").

¶ The Inventory of Simon Geslin, 13th April 1769 (*Ibid.*).

worker is better able to detect any faults in her work upon a coloured ground than upon white. The paper pattern is laid upon the strip of parchment, which rests on a pillow, and the outlines of the ornament are pricked with a needle. After pricking, the parchment is given to a *traceuse*, who first sews it to a piece of very coarse linen folded double, then forms the outline of the pattern by two threads,* which are guided along the edge by the thumb of the left hand, and fixed by minute stitches passed with another needle and thread through the holes of the parchment. The "picage" and the "trace" date in Alençon from the first imitation of points de Venise. The next process, the making of the "fond" or "entoilage,"† employs exactly the same stitch which was used for the mat of point coupé and for the "flowers" of point de Venise. The worker works the button-hole stitch (point bouclé or de boutonnière, not, as is stated in so many authors, point noué) from left to right, and when arrived at the end of the row, the thread is thrown back to the point of departure, and she works again from left to right over the thread. Occasionally small pin-holes (portes) or a diaper pattern of pin-holes (quadrilles) were let into the fond. A more open variety of the fond is the rempli,‡ formed by twisting the thread before making the loop, and these two processes were at first executed by the same worker.

The brides of Alençon are of three sorts—the bride à picots, the bride bouclée, and the bride tortillée. The first—the bride à picots— had, in later point de Venise, shown a tendency to approximate to a regular, generally hexagonal, mesh. These brides in Alençon were not marked upon the parchment until the reign of Louis XVI., and were made at sight, and towards the middle of the reign of

---

* "D'abord on se servit de deux fils doubles ce qui arrive quelquefois obtenir une trace solide" ("Histoire du Point d'Alençon").

† "Les brides étants presque nulles, on commençait ordinairement un morceau par les motifs. C'est pour cette raison que ce point porta dès l'origine le nom de fond, nom qui aurait dû appartenir aux brides et plus tard au réseau. Il conserva cependant ce nom de fond, et de nos jours il sert encore à designer le mat des fleures, feuilles, ou autres ornements réservés à cet effet" (*Ibid.*).

‡ The rempli is found in point coupé, and used as contrast to the fond, employed for closer effect.

Plate LXXII.

LAPPET OF ARGENTAN.
Louis XVI., late eighteenth century.

LAPPET OF ALENÇON.
Louis XV., eighteenth century.

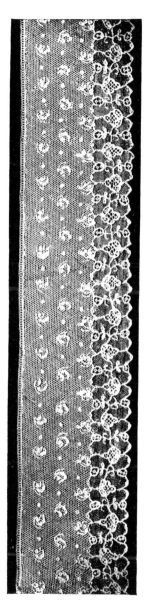

BORDER OR EDGING OF ALENÇON.
Louis XVI., late eighteenth century. The réseau is of thick thread, a deteriorated and later substitute for the small hexagonal "brides" ground.

Plate LXXIII.

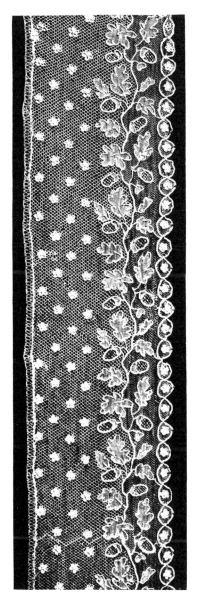

BORDER OF ALENÇON.
Louis XVI., late eighteenth century.

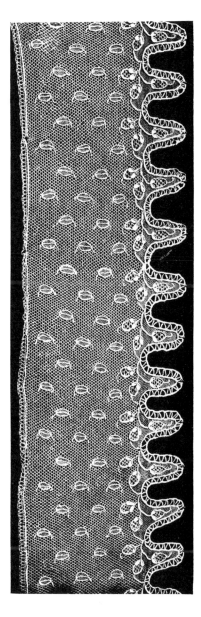

BORDER OF ALENÇON.
Empire, early nineteenth century.

Louis XIV. the meshes show an exact hexagonal form. It will be remembered that in 1673 the "nouveau point de Paris" is described in the *Mercure* as covered with "an infinite number of small picots." The bride bouclée sans nez, also an hexagonal mesh, has no picots, and was invented about 1700. In the bride tortillée the mesh is covered with a thread twisted round it, and held in place by a button-hole stitch at each angle.*

The réseau is worked from left to right, au point bouclé et tortillé, with the thread attached to the outline of the flowers and ornaments.† It began to be made at Alençon about 1700, as Madame Despierres proves from various inventories,‡ and not as Mrs Palliser and M. Séguin assert, in 1741 at the earliest. The modes are made, like reticella, upon skeleton foundations of thread, which are afterwards covered with button-hole stitches, and were introduced, when the réseau was used, to give an open and clear effect to certain portions of the design. The first modes were varieties of the brides à picots and zigzag bars picoted (Les Venises). The modes of Alençon, though very light, open, and effective, are not so rich and varied as those in Venise à réseau, or Brussels lace. Indeed, in 1761, a writer, describing the point de France, says that it does not arrive at the taste and delicacy of Brussels, and that the modes are inferior, and consequently much point is sent from Alençon to Brussels to have the modes added ; but connoisseurs, he adds, easily detect the difference.§ A favourite mode is the square trellis foundation, ornamented with squares and circles at the points of intersection. Zigzag lines finely picoted are also used with effect. One of the modes, which consists of a button-hole stitched solid hexagon within a skeleton hexagon,‖

* "On plaçait autrefois une épingle au haut de chaque hexagone, afin d'obtenir une tension pour la forme regulière de la maille, lorsque l'on se servait d'épingles, elle s'appelait bride épinglée" ("Histoire du Point d'Alençon").

† There are several varieties of réseau—le réseau ordinaire, le petit réseau, le réseau mouché, le réseau avec bobine, le grand réseau.

‡ "Le réseau se fait dans le sens du pied de la dentelle à son bord, par rangs de gauche à droite, au point bouclé et tortillé peu serré. Lorsque le rang est fini on revient en passant trois fois son aiguille dans chaque maille, et l'on recommence la deuxième rang de la même manière" ("Histoire du Point d'Alençon").

§ "Dictionnaire du Citoyen," Paris, 1761.

‖ It is sometimes set within a square.

and connected with the surrounding figure by means of six small ties or brides, is sometimes used extensively to form a groundwork, when it has been named by M. Dupont Auberville, "réseau rosacé" (Argentella). This "Argentella" was supposed by Mrs Palliser to be of Genoese* workmanship, but it has no affinities with the type of lace made in Genoa, while its character and the style of the floral patterns are those of Alençon. Its cordonnet† is worked in button-hole stitches closely cast over a thread, which outlines various forms in the design —a distinctive mark of point d'Alençon. In general the laces distinguished as point d'Alençon, point d'Argentan, and Argentella have so many characteristics in common that it would be preferable to call them Alençon à réseau, Alençon à grandes brides, and Alençon à réseau rosacé.

La brode,‡ the next process, is worked in button-hole stitch, and gives relief to the design in the veining of the leaves, the stalks of the flowers, &c. The brode is borrowed by Alençon from raised Venetian point, but the relief is much lower in the French brode. To obtain the raised effect, a pad of coarse thread was laid down, and upon these very close button-hole stitches were worked. When this is completed, the threads which unite lace, parchment, and linen are cut by a sharp razor passed between the two folds of linen; the loose threads are removed (enlevage and eboutage), the *regaleuse* repairs any small defects, and there remains one last process,§ that of uniting all the segments of lace imperceptibly together, or the "assemblage." The seam follows as much as possible the outlines of

---

* "Formerly much of it was to be met with in the curiosity shops of that city" (Mrs Palliser, 1864).

† The cordonnet is sometimes of stout thread.

‡ "La brodeuse . . . attache à sa ceinture un fil appelé menu ou fil conducteur, puis elle attache un autre fil à la trace. Elle fait sur le menu trois ou quatres points bouclés, fiche son aiguille dans la trace en faisant le quatrième ou le cinquième point, et continue, en procédant toujours de la même manière" ("Histoire du Point d'Alençon").

§ "L'assemblage consiste à raccorder les dessins, à les unir par une cousure quand c'est une fleur. Lorsqu'il s'agit du champ, soit de bride, soit de réseau, on refait les mailles, afin que l'assemblage ne paraisse pas. C'est toujours une ouvrière habile que l'on choisit pour ce travail. L'assembleuse doit connaître tous les points."

Plate LXXIV.

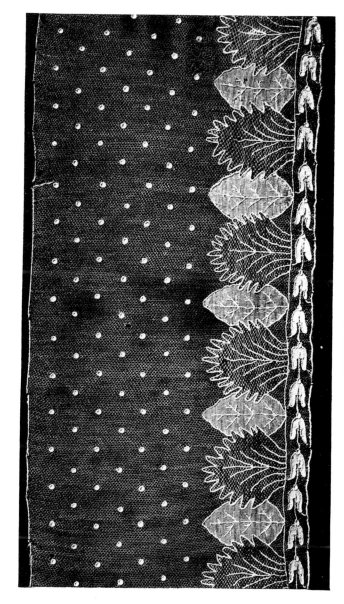

FLOUNCE OF ALENÇON.
Empire, early nineteenth century.

()

Plate LXXV.

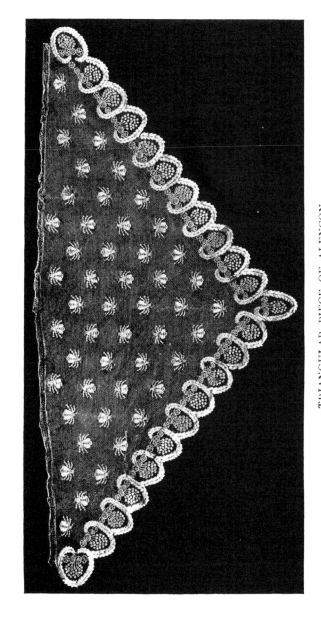

TRIANGULAR PIECE OF ALENÇON.   Empire, about 1810.

The ground powdered with the Napoleonic bees; said to have belonged to the Empress Marie Louise.

the pattern. When finished, a steel instrument, the *aficot*, was passed into each flower to polish it and remove any inequalities on its surface. There are therefore twelve processes, including the design. These can be subdivided into twenty or twenty-two.

In point d'Alençon horsehair was introduced to give firmness and consistency to the cordonnet in the later period of Louis XV., and during the reign of Louis XVI. It has been objected * that this cordonnet thickens when put into water, and that the horsehair edge draws up the flower from the ground, and makes it rigid and heavy. It was this solidity of Alençon, and of the still heavier Argentan which caused them to be known as "dentelles d'hiver." † According to Peuchet, it was only worn in the winter, though at that date it was sufficiently light in design.

In 1836 Baron Mercier, thinking by producing it at a lower price to procure a more favourable sale, set up a lace school, and caused the girls to work the patterns on bobbin net, as bearing some resemblance to the old point de bride, but fashion did not favour point de bride, so the plan failed. The only important modern innovator in workmanship was the introduction of "shading" on the flowers by M. Beaumé in 1855. Shaded tints were brought in tentatively by M. Larnaz Triboult, and in a book of patterns for point made between 1811 and 1814, certain leaves were marked to be shaded. This effect is made by varying the application of the two stitches used in making the flowers—the toilé, which forms the closer tissue, and the grillé, the more open part of the pattern. This system has been adopted in France, Belgium, and England, but with most success in France. The thread from which Alençon was made was spun at Lille,‡ and also at Mechlin and Nouvion.

---

* "Dictionnaire du Citoyen," Paris, 1761.

† "Déjà, sous Louis XV., le point d'Alençon et le point d'Argentan étaient designés par l'etiquette come 'dentelles d'hiver'" (C. Blanc, "L'Art dans la Parure").

‡ "La fabrique de Lille fournit les fils pour le travail du point. Ils sont plus fins et plus retors que les fils destinés à la plus fine dentelle" ("Dictionnaire Universel de la Géographie Commerçante," 1789).

Argentan Lace.

Of all the point de France centres, Alençon, with its neighbour Argentan (the two towns are separated by some ten miles), produced the most brilliant and the most permanent results; and at Argentan, which has been mentioned in 1664 as having long learned the art of imitating points de Venise, a bureau for the manufactures of points de France was established at the same time as the bureau of Alençon. Early Argentan no doubt produced point of the same type as that of Alençon, and the two laces only began to be distinguished when Alençon adopted the réseau ground.

"Argentan" is the term given to lace (whether made at Alençon or Argentan) with large bride ground, which consists of a six-sided mesh, worked over with button-hole stitches. "It was always printed on the parchment pattern, and the upper angle of the hexagon was pricked; the average side of a diagonal taken from angle to angle, in a so-called Argentan hexagon, was about one-sixth of an inch, and each side of the hexagon was about one-tenth of an inch. An idea of the minuteness of the work can be formed from the fact that a side of a hexagon would be overcast with some nine or ten button-hole stitches."

In other details, the workmanship of the laces styled Alençon and Argentan is identical; the large bride ground, however, could support a flower bolder and larger in pattern, in higher and heavier relief, than the réseau ground.

Peuchet writes in the late eighteenth century that the bride ground of Argentan was preferred in France, and that the workmanship of Argentan was superior to that of Alençon: "Elles ont de beaux dessins pour le fond, et pour la regularité des yeux, de la bride et du réseau." He adds that lace was sent from Alençon to Argentan to have the modes made and also the fond and the bride ground.

"The two towns had communications as frequent as those which passed between Alençon and the little village of Vimoutier, eighteen miles distant, where one workman in particular produced what is known as the true Alençon lace."* As Peuchet writes, the "fabricants"

* A. S. Cole.

Plate LXXVI.

BORDER OF ARGENTAN.   Early eighteenth century.

The upper portion being filled in with a grounding of réseau rosacé, the lower with the Argentan ground.

of Alençon* could have the fond and the bride bouclée made by the workwoman employed by the "fabricants" of Argentan. At Alençon all the varieties of bride and réseau were made, while at Argentan a speciality was made of the bride ground.†

The bride picotée—a survival of the early Venetian teaching—was also a speciality in Argentan point. It consists of the hexagonal button-holed bride, ornamented with three or four picots. The secret of making it was entirely lost by 1869.‡

Towards the beginning of the eighteenth century, when the manufacture had fallen into decay, it was raised in 1708 by one Sieur Mathieu Guyard, a merchant mercer, who states that "his ancestors and himself had more than one hundred and twenty years been occupied in fabricating black silk and white thread lace in the environs of Paris."

In 1729, Monthulay, another manufacturer, presented the contrôleur général, M. Lepeltier des Forts, with a piece of point *without any raised work*, representing the contrôleur's arms §—a novel departure in the fabric. The fabric was checked by the Revolution, and died out after a short revival in 1810. In 1858 Argentan point had become rare, and the introduction of cotton about 1830, instead of the linen thread from Lille, Mechlin, and Nouvion debased its quality.

The design for Alençon and Argentan is identical, though its

---

* " On vient même d'Alençon faire faire des brides et des fonds à Argentan et on y achève des modes."

† " Les trois sortes de brides comme champ sont exécutées dans les deux fabriques, et les points ont été et sont encore faits par les mêmes procédés de fabrication, et avec les mêmes matières textiles " (" Histoire du Point d'Alençon ").

‡ In January 1874, with the assistance of the Mayor, M. Lefébure made a search in the greniers of the Hôtel Dieu, and discovered three specimens of point d'Argentan in progress on the parchment patterns. " One was of bold pattern with the grande bride ground, evidently a man's ruffle; the other had the barette or bride ground of point de France; the third picoted, showing that the three descriptions of lace were made contemporaneously at Argentan" (Mrs Palliser, "History of Lace").

§ " Histoire du Point d'Alençon."

sequence is more easily studied in the more important manufacture of Alençon.

As M. Paul Lecroix has observed, France never failed to put her own stamp on whatever she adopted, thus making any fashion essentially French, even though she had only just borrowed it from Spain, England, Germany, or Italy.

This is especially true of French needlepoint lace, of which the technicalities and design were borrowed *en bloc* from Italy. Gradually, however, the French taste superseded the Italian treatment, and produced a style which, no doubt, owed much of its perfection and consistency to the State patronage it enjoyed and to the position of artistic design in France, a fact which was noticed early in the eighteenth century by Bishop Berkeley. " How," he asks, "could France and Flanders have drawn so much money from other countries for figured silk, lace, and tapestry if they had not had their academies of design ?"

During the Louis XIV. period, until the last fifteen years of the reign, points de France were made with the bride ground, and to judge by the evidence of portraits, preserved in general the rolling scroll of Venetian rose points. Some specimens, however, show a French influence in the composition of the design, a tendency which (as when expressed in textiles, or metal) led to a style of symmetrical composition, with fantastic shapes. A certain " architectural " arrangement, and the use of canopies, with scroll devices on either side of them which Bérain uses, is certainly met with in lace. An ornament consisting of two S's, *addorsed*, and surmounted by a miniature canopy, is of not uncommon occurrence, and also a somewhat grotesque cock, and a small fleur-de-lys or trefoil. The king's monogram, the interlaced L's, and the *flamme d'amour* arising from two hearts are also met with, a compliment of the royal manufacture to its royal patron.

There are some good specimens of point de France in the Musée des Arts Décoratifs at Paris. Two very interesting specimens of point de France are in the collection of Madame Porgès, and were exhibited at the Exposition Internationale of 1900 at Paris. The first, a fragment, has as central motif the sun in splendour surmounted by a dome or dome-shaped canopy, flanked by two trophies of crossed swords and flags. Another piece in the same collection has a young

Plate LXXVII.

FLOUNCE OF ARGENTAN.

Louis XV., eighteenth century (much reduced).   (*In the possession of Mrs Finch.*)

man attired as an antique warrior wearing a huge helmet with the double eagle as a crest. Above his head is the closed crown of a royal prince, supported by two angels. Above this crown again is a small Bacchus astride a wine-cask. The motif of two dolphins suggests that the piece represents the Dauphin, the son of Louis XIV. Two Indians, with the conventional kilt and upstanding crown of feathers, offer the warrior flowers. Below are the Dauphin's two sons, the Duc de Burgogne and the Duc d'Anjou, as young warriors, crowned by flying genii. The Dauphin treads upon a characteristic trophy of arms, cannon, and standards.

In a Swiss collection there is a somewhat later piece, a square cravat end, in the centre of which is a lady seated at an organ ; beneath an ornate canopy various figures play various musical instruments—a lyre, a violin, a violoncello, castanets—while two figures sing, holding a music-book. Light, fantastic, short scrolls fill up the ground. Two somewhat similar cravats in the Victoria and Albert Museum (Bolckow Bequest) have, among various motifs, a draped and scalloped canopy above the figure of a lady in full toilette seated upon a bird with displayed plumage. Below her is a fantastic pedestal with balanced rococo and leafy shapes on each side of it ; immediately above the flanking shapes are small figures in Oriental costume. On the upper right and left of this central group is the half-figure of a lady with a cockatoo in one piece, and the half-figure of a lady with a little dog under her arm in the other. Below, to right and left of the large central group, is a smaller vertical group of a flower vase on stand with blossoms radiating from it, and beneath this is a gentleman playing a violoncello and a lady playing a musical instrument. All these objects are held together by small bars or brides à picots (Plate LXVI.).

In Venetian rose-point laces of the same period, probably owing to French influence, design became more frequently vertical and balanced upon either side of an imaginary central line. At the end of Louis XIV.'s reign lace in cravats, ruffles, and flounces was worn fuller * or in folds, a hanging pattern, or one in which the arrangement of details

---

* "A la fin du règne de Louis XIV. les rabats ne se portaient plus à plat mais froncés sous le nom de cravates" (Lefébure).

was conspicuously vertical,* was found more appropriate than horizontal arrangements of ornament which require to lie flat. This symmetrical tendency owes something to the personal taste of Louis XIV. Madame de Maintenon writes in one of her letters that the king was so fond of symmetry in his architecture that he would have people "perish in his symmetry"; for he caused his doors and windows to be constructed in pairs opposite to one another, "which gave everybody who lived in his palaces their death of cold from draughts."

A specimen of early point de France of this period, where the vertical arrangement is most noticeable, is No. 747, 1870, in the Victoria and Albert Museum, a tablier of needlepoint lace scalloped with patterns of pine-apples, flowers, leaves, and conventional forms upon a hexagonal ground of bride à picots. Another very early piece is No. 552, 1868, of the same collection, a large scrolling design upon a hexagonal bride ground.

The former specimen shows a tendency, which later distinguishes French design, to the planning of the lines of the design upon a conventional basis, while treating the detail somewhat naturalistically.† Lace, which is largely influenced by contemporary textiles and embroidery, was not without its influence upon certain brocades and silks of the Louis XIV. period, where small trellisings and spots like the à jours so generally introduced in the larger pieces of lace, are met with. ‡

---

* This vertical arrangement may be noticed in certain French portraits, as, for example, in the point lace in the portrait of the Duchesse de Nemours, by Hyacinthe Rigaud.

† In French brocades of the seventeenth century the shapes of the flowers and leaves are more detached from one another and distinctly depicted than those of contemporary Italian patterns.

‡ "In a piece of satin and coloured silk brocade, period Louis XIV., French, late seventeenth century, the bands forming the ogees are broad and elaborated with small trellisings and spots, which lace fanciers will recognise as being very similar to the à jours so frequently introduced into the large point de France, point d'Alencon, and point d'Argentan of the later years of the seventeenth and earlier years of the eighteenth centuries. A greater variety of effects arising from this

Plate LXXVIII.

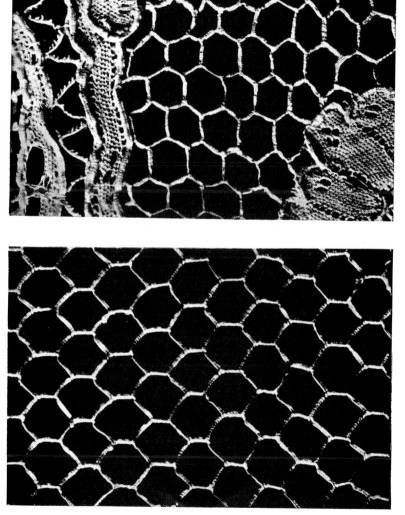

PIECE OF ARGENTAN LACE.
Enlarged, showing *toilé* and cordonnet.

ARGENTAN MESH.
Enlarged.

The réseau ground, introduced about 1700, naturally introduced a finer, more minute floral genre of design, and a new style began to declare itself, associated with the reign of Louis XV. Here, as in furniture and decoration generally, the symmetrical tendency was overthrown and oblique and slanted motifs were the fashion. The impoverishment of the kingdom towards the end of the reign had had its effect upon trade. Many manufactures had disappeared, and those remaining lost two-thirds of their custom. A more simple and saleable genre of lace was substituted for the important pieces of Louis XIV.'s reign. As the design became thinner the réseau ground filled up its deficiencies, while to give it "interest" enclosures of a finer ground were introduced and à jours filled with light and open patterns.

The floral patterns of the period no doubt result from the fact that French designers had from very early times peculiar encouragement to draw and paint from plant forms of great variety, which were cultivated in public gardens. French textile patterns of the seventeenth century are full of effects derived from a close adherence to natural forms, the expression of which pervades their art in a more lively and dainty manner than in the corresponding Italian patterns. Yet another motif introduced into lace from textiles is the Louis XV. wavy ribbon pattern, generally enclosing a rich variety of grounds. The twining ribbon patterns encircling flowers within their spiral volutions were amongst the most popular products of the Lyons factories at the close of the seventeenth century. Tocqué's portrait of Marie Leczinska (1740) shows that a pattern of sprays of flowers entwined in a double serpentine ribbon or ribbon-like convolution was fashionable at that date.

The ribbon motif may often be seen in its usual form of undulating lines, dividing the ground into oval compartments, from which a spray or flower springs. The introduction of military "trophies" is not unusual. Cannons and flags are sometimes skilfully combined with floral ornament.

Certain exotic features and "chinoiseries" are to be noted in lace as characteristically French adaptation of lace devices is given in the embellishment of the leaves and flowers of a piece of olive-green satin damask woven in white silk" (A. S. Cole, "Ornament in European Silks").

in the decoration of the late seventeenth and early eighteenth centuries. The appearance of Indian figures in lace is a curious reflection of the taste of the time. Such figures invariably show the odd kilt-like skirt reaching to the knees, and on the head a circlet of upstanding feathers of the conventional savage of the period ; sometimes a hunting implement is slung across the shoulder. Other figures of a pseudo-Oriental character are also to be found—a pendant to the taste which demanded negro attendants, Oriental lacquer plaques inlaid upon furniture, and Indian gods in the boudoirs.

In textiles design towards the latter part of the eighteenth century became still more simplified.* Alternating straight stripes and bands running vertically up and down the pattern are mingled with small bunches of flowers, sometimes with tiny detached sprays and spots. "C'est le ligne droite qui domine!"† These straight stripes, which appeared towards the last year of Louis XVI., were retained during the Republic and the Consulate. It is interesting to note that the output of examples of this type coincides in point of time with the period when the finances of France were suffering considerably from the extravagances both of the Government and of individuals during the reigns of Louis XIV. and XV.‡ Lace follows closely the developments of textiles. (See lappet in Plate LXXII.)

In lace, instead of wreaths, ribbons, or festoons undulating from one side of the border to another, we have a stiff rectilinear border of purely conventional design, the reflection of the dominant straight line of decoration.§ In textiles also, as in lace, semés become more widely separated.

In lace, under Louis XVI., it became the fashion to multiply the number of flounces to dresses and to gather them into pleats, so that ornamental motifs, more or less broken up or partially concealed by the pleats, lost their significance and *flow*. The general ornamental

---

* M. Dupont-Auberville, " L'Ornement des Tissus."

† Rouaix, " Les Styles."

‡ A. S. Cole, " Ornament in European Silks."

§ The straight line in furniture was the result of the revival of " classic " taste and imitation of classic models.

effect of the lace of the period depended upon the orderly repetition and arrangement of the same details over and over again. The spaces between the motifs widened more and more until the design deteriorated into semés of small devices, detached flowers, pois, larmes, fleurons, rosettes. The design usually only ran along the edge of a piece of lace, the upper portion was réseau, little disguised * (Plate LXXIV.).

The prevalent fashion in costume of the period did not exact such ornamental elaboration of laces as had distinguished even the preceding reign.† An illustration of the diminishing use of lace is a portrait by Drouais, of Turgot (1778), showing but a small ruffle or edging to his shirt front instead of the full folds of a deep cravat. A great deal of lace of this date is straight-edged, and shows two grounds, the finer réseau as a border, and a coarser variety for the upper portion covered with a very simple design or semé. The minute picots on the condonnets of the little sprays of flowers and ornament of the lace of this period should be noticed. The sharp, thin appearance of the work is chiefly due to the use of fine horsehair used as the foundation line of the cordonnet of every ornament, upon which the fine threads have been cast. In earlier Alençon the horsehair was used along the border of the piece only.

The Empire style follows with its decided phase of heavy classicalism. At first the small semé was used, but instead of the rose and tulip leaves, laurel and olive leaves were substituted. In lace, Roman emblems and attributes were introduced, and the Napoleonic bee appears on some pieces of Alençon specially made for Marie Louise. A triangular piece of Brussels vrai réseau of this set with bees of Alençon point is shown in the illustration (Plate LXXV.).

---

* Compare the last lace bill of Madame du Barry, 1773 : "Une paire de barbes plattes longues de 3/4 en blonde fine à fleurs fond d'Alençon. Une blonde grande hauteur à bouquets détachés et à bordure riche. 6 au de blonde de grande hauteur façon d'Alençon à coquilles à mille poix."

† According to Wraxall ("Memoirs," ed. 1815, i. 138), the total abolition of buckles and ruffles was not made till the era of Jacobinism and of equality in 1793 and 1794. Sir P. J. Clerk, though a strong Whig, wore "very rich laced ruffles" as late as 1781.

Large spaces of réseau with semés and a straight-edged border continued in fashion (Plate LXXIV.).

In the Porgès Collection are one or two Empire pieces showing coats-of-arms, garlands, and draperies held up by cords and tassels, and the foliage of the oak and laurel ornament, the lace destined for the wives of the Chevaliers of the Legion of Honour.

The laces of the Restoration are heavy and tasteless.

CHAPTER XIII.

LILLE AND ARRAS.

LILLE.

LACE was made at Lille,* the ancient capital of Flanders, in 1582, but as it has been a French town since the Treaty of Aix-la-Chapelle in 1668,† and Nimeguen (1678), its productions are included among French laces, though in character and design they are more closely allied to those of Flanders.

Peuchet mentions the products of Lille in the "genre" of Mechlin and Valenciennes, and says that much "fausse Valenciennes," very like the "vraie" type, was fabricated in the hospital at Lille.

The design in Lille of the late eighteenth and early nineteenth centuries resembles Mechlin, the special difference between the two laces lying in the make of the réseau. The Lille ground, fine, light, and transparent, has a hexagonal mesh, and is called "fond clair," or "fond simple." "Four sides of the mesh are formed by twisting two threads round each other, and the remaining two sides by simple crossing of the threads over each other." Square dots ("points d'esprit") are one of the characteristics of Lille, as are also the straight edge, and light, formal pattern, outlined by a coarse, flat, untwisted linen thread, which shows up against the very transparent fond clair,

---

* "Cette ville possédait autrefois plusieurs industries d'art très prospères ; la dentelle, la tapisserie, l'impression sur tissus. Les traditions artistiques flamandes leur avaient conservé une grande originalité" (Marius Vachon, "Les Industries d'Art," Nancy, 1897).

† At this time a number of lace-workers withdrew from Lille to Ghent.

and the oval openings left near the edge of the lace, and filled in with simple à jours.

In 1803 the price of thread having risen 30 per cent., the lace-makers, unwilling to raise the prices of their lace, adopted a larger mesh, in order to diminish the quantity of thread required.

ARRAS.

" Arras, from the earliest ages, has been a working city ; the nuns of the convent excelled in all kinds of needlework," and lace-making was in 1602 the principal occupation of the institution of the Filles de Sainte-Agnès.   M. de Cardevacque, in his " Histoire de la Dentelle d'Arras," gives some curious details of the methods of teaching lace-making in these conventual establishments, the pupils beginning with bobbin lace in which only four bobbins were employed.

Owing to its early repute as a centre of bobbin lace, Arras was chosen as an establishment of the points de France, and Valenciennes were copied there with some success in 1713.*

In the later eighteenth century, Arras, like Lille, made a quantity of narrow light lace, which went by the name of " mignonette," which was very popular during the Empire (1804-12), since which period it has declined.   In 1800, the laces of Lille and Arras were the only "dentelles communes" in vogue, and their strength, whiteness, and low price assured them a market.

---

* " Les dentelles qui se fabriquent à Arras dans la maison de la Providence et qui passent pour être assez belles, ne sont qu'une copie de celles de Valenciennes, et les ouvrières les exécutent très lentement " (" Letter of M. de Bernage, Intendant at Amiens to the Contrôleur-général," 3rd and 7th May 1713).

Plate LXXIX.

EDGINGS OR BORDERS OF LILLE.

CHAPTER XIV.

CHANTILLY.

CHANTILLY, in the department of Oise, is the centre of a district long famous for its silk laces, in black and white, the manufacture having been established in the seventeenth century by the Duchesse de Longueville; the name of a lace-maker, Charlotte Martin, is mentioned in 1700, and about 1750 there were three houses of lace-dealers, Moreau, Le Tellier, and Lionnet.*

Chantilly black lace has always been made of silk, but from its being a grenadine, not a shining silk, a common error prevails that it is thread, whereas black thread lace has never been made either at Chantilly or Bayeux. In the inventories of the eighteenth century black lace and black silk lace appears fairly frequently. A specimen illustrated in the "History of Lace" from an old order-book of the time of Louis XVI. shows a straight-edged lace with a flower-vase design, the flowers worked in grillé or open stitch, the pattern outlined with a cordonnet. In the Victoria and Albert Museum, No. 868, 1853, is a piece of lace with a flower-pot pattern, and the fond chant ground of the eighteenth century. A piece in the Musée des Arts Décoratifs, Paris, is exactly like that illustrated from the old order-book of the time of Louis XVI. The designs of this period were "vases" or "flowering" baskets, small ornaments, small flowers, "pois" arranged like pearls on a string.

Like other French fabrics, Chantilly suffered in the Revolution, and had a short period of comparative prosperity under the Empire. In

* G. H. Quignon, "La Dentelle Chantilly."

1805, the Chantilly workwomen made white blonde, which was then in fashion in Paris ; and large patterned blondes were also made for exportation to Spain and her American colonies.

The lace industry has been driven away from Chantilly by the increase in the price of labour consequent on its vicinity to the capital, and by the competition of Calvados.

The grounds used in Chantilly were the Alençon ground, and the fond chant (an abbreviation of Chantilly), or six-pointed star réseau.*

Chantilly, in the early nineteenth century, was exported to Holland, Russia, Germany, Portugal, and England.   After 1827, the trade considerably declined, and its decadence was further accentuated from 1830-40.

Until 1840 Chantilly was made in bands from 10 to 12 centimètres wide, which were afterwards invisibly joined.   After 1840, in the reign of Louis Philippe, Chantilly came into favour, and large pieces were designed, often made in one piece, fichus, shawls, and later "barbes." In the reign of Napoleon III. very ambitious and remarkable specimens of Chantilly were produced, the ornament delicately "shaded."   In 1870, the lace houses became bankrupt somewhat suddenly, many parchments and unfinished pieces of lace were left in the hands of the workers and never claimed, and a great deal of Chantilly was sold at a loss to the Prussians during the siege of Paris.

Le Puy produced† from 1850 to 1870 lace like Chantilly, but with the fond chant ground instead of the fond d'Alençon. ‡

To the collector looking for Chantilly, a few hints will be useful. It is more difficult to distinguish between real and machine-made lace in black than in white (as the colour and texture of linen thread and cotton are very distinct in white).   A fairly safe test is the edge. In the case of real Chantilly, the loops on the edge will be found to be part of the lace, but in the machine-made lace, these will be found to be sewn on, and can easily be pulled away.   In general, the weakest point of all machine-made lace is its edge.

* 1787, "Une paire de barbes de dentelle noire Alençon à bordure longue" ("Livre-Journal de Madame Eloffe," ed. the Comte de Reiset).

† Modern Chantilly lace is no longer made at Chantilly itself, but at Calvados, Caen, and Bayeux.

‡ Chantilly was imitated in Belgium at Grammont, but the black lace is too soft and without consistency ; the silk used for the ornament was too fine.

Plate LXXX.

VEIL OF BLACK CHANTILLY LACE.

Nineteenth century.

With the better imitation this is always the case, especially in the needle-run, which is the nearest to the genuine pillow-made article ; in this the net and design are made on the machine, there the gimp or outlining of the design is run in by hand—hence the term needle-run lace.

In the commoner makes the loops at the edge will often be found to have been cut, owing to the carelessness of the operator in dividing the strips when taken from the loom, settling at once that it is of no value.*

* Note by a correspondent in the *Connoisseur*, November 1905.

CHAPTER XV.

ENGLISH NEEDLEPOINT.

IT has been said that originality has never been a marked feature of English needlework, and that at all times its patterns and stitches have shown well-defined traces of foreign influence; also skilful adaptation rather than invention has distinguished its executants even when the art has been at its highest· level in this country. This is entirely true with regard to the English needlepoint laces of the early seventeenth century, in which the design and the method of workmanship is that of the contemporary Italian work. The fine flax for lacemaking was also not home-grown, but imported from Flanders * and France. According to Fuller not a tenth part of the flax used in England was home-grown.†

* "If the law made for sowing hemp and flax were executed and . . . provision made for growing woad and madder in the realm, as by some men's diligence it is already practised, which growth is here found better than that from beyond seas, we should not need to seek into France for it. Besides Flanders hath enough; no country robbeth England so much as France" ("Considerations delivered to the Parliament, 1559," "Calendar of Cecil MSS.," Part I., Hist. MSS. Comm.).

† Lydgate, in "Ballad of London Luckpenny," writes that Paris thread was the most prized :

"Here is Paris thredde, the finest in the land."

"Our whole land (doth not) afford the tenth part of what is spent therein ; so that we are fain to fetch it from Flanders, France, yea as far as Egypt itself. It may seem strange that our soil kindly for that seed, the use whereof and profit hereby so great, yet so little care is taken for the planting thereof, which well husbanded would find linen for the rich and living for the poor. Many would never be indicted spinsters, were they *spinsters* indeed. . . . Some thousands of pounds are sent yearly over out of England to buy that commodity" (Fuller, "Worthies of England").

Plate LXXXI.

PORTRAIT OF LADY ELIZABETH PAULET.
(*Ashmolean Gallery, Oxford.*)

Cutwork, described as of Italian and Flemish manufacture, the former being the more expensive, is of common occurrence in Queen Elizabeth's Wardrobe Accounts, and an English version of Vinciolo * was printed in 1591, in which we are told that cutwork was "greatly accepted of by ladies and gentlemen, and consequently by the common people." An illustration from the Ashmolean Gallery, Oxford, shows a fine apron † of cutwork, perhaps made by the wearer, Lady Elizabeth Paulet, who holds in her left hand a small picture of the Magdalen, probably in needlework. It is attributed to Daniel Mytens the elder (d. 1656), who painted in England in the reigns of James I. and Charles I. The *English Connoisseur* (ii. 80) mentions a "Lady Betty Paulet, an ingenious lady of the Duke of Bolton's family in the reign of James I., *drawn in a dress of her own work*, full length," probably the same "Lady Eliz. Paulet" whose gift of certain admirable needlework was accepted by the University·of Oxford in convocation, 9th July 1636‡ (Plate LXXXI.).

When needlepoint lace forsook purely geometrical lines, certain English characteristics are noticeable. In the Victoria and Albert Museum a pair of scallops of needlepoint lace contain within one compartment a thistle, within the other a rose, and there are two of similar design in Mr Sydney Vacher's collection (Plate LXXXV.). In the interesting collar described as Italian in the Victoria and Albert Museum, the design is of flowers arranged stiffly on an angular stem. These flowers, Tudor roses and pinks, are more naturalistic than any

---

* " New and Singular Patterns and Workes of Linnen serving for Patternes to make all sorts of Lace Edginges and Cutworkes," by Vincentio. Printed by John Wolfe and Edward White, 1591. In the "Epistle to the Reader" we have its foreign origin admitted : " It being my chance to lighten upon certaine paternes of cutworke and others brought out of foreign countries which have bin greatly accepted of by divers ladies and gentlewomen of sundrie nations, and consequently of the common people," &c.

† A similar apron, composed almost entirely of geometrical lace, is seen in the portrait of Anne, daughter of Sir Peter Vanlore, Kt., first wife of Sir Charles Cæsar, Kt. (about 1614), in the possession of Captain Cottrell-Dormer. This portrait is the frontispiece of the " History of Lace," Mrs Palliser, ed. 1902. The lace is there stated to be probably Flemish.

‡ Many of the verses written in her honour by Cartwright and others have been preserved. In the Bodleian a volume of them is MS. Bodl. 22.

in Italian lace, and the Tudor rose, with stiff opposite leaflets, is not infrequently to be found in English samplers. The raised free petals of the rose are also characteristic.* The design also is compact and closely crowded, showing no feeling of the value of background so characteristic in Italian lace. Somewhat similar qualities may be seen in the collar of needlepoint in the picture of James Harrington (author of " Oceana "), by Gerard Honthorst, in the National Portrait Gallery, and various other portraits of the reign of Charles I. The somewhat torn collar from the Isham Collection in the Victoria and Albert Museum is of the same type, close, compact, and thick (Plate LXXXII.). In the same collection is a boy's doublet of white linen, quilted and embroidered with gold coloured silk, and edged with needlepoint lace.

In 1635 a royal proclamation, having for its object the protection of home fabrics, prohibited the use of foreign cutworks, and ordered all "purles," † cutworks, and "bone laces" of English make to be taken to a house "near the sign of the Red Hart, in Fore Street, without Cripplegate, and then sealed by Thomas Smith or his deputy."

Needlepoint lace representing some Bible story is occasionally to be met with in samplers of the seventeenth century. A sachet in the possession of Sir Hubert Jerningham shows Salome, with the head of John the Baptist, before Herod. The dresses are picked out with seed pearls, and the eyes indicated by small black beads. A similar but larger specimen is in the possession of Mrs Head, and represents the Judgment of Solomon. A third piece in the possession of Mrs

---

* In a coverlet, No. 348, 1901, in the Victoria and Albert Museum, some of the petals of the floral sprays embroidered upon it have been separately worked, and afterwards fixed to the satin, so as to stand away from the ground—an attempt at realism characteristic of English work.

† Purl is to form an edging on lace, to form an embroidered border. It is a contraction of the old word *purfle*, to embroider on the edge. M.E. *purfilen*, Old French *porfiler*, later *pourfiler*. " *Pourfiler d'or*, to purfle, tinsell, or overcast with gold thread (Cotgrave)."

"*Lace*, a cord, tie, plaited string (F., —L.), M.E. *las*, *laas*, King Alisaunder, 7698 ; Chaucer, C.T. 394—O.F. *las*, *lags*, a snare ; *cf.* lags courant, a noose, running knot (Cot.)—Lat. *laqueus*, a noose, snare or knot " (Skeat).

Plate LXXXII.

MAN'S FALLING COLLAR.

With a broad scalloped border of English reticella (cutwork), and *punto in aria*.　About 1630-40.

Plate LXXXIII.

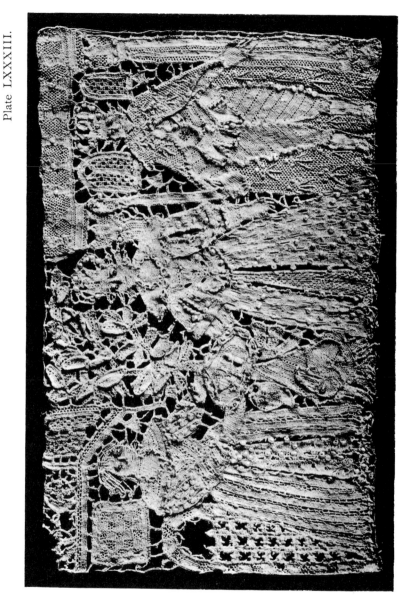

OBLONG PIECE OF ENGLISH NEEDLEPOINT.

Representing Salome, Herodias, and Herod.　Early seventeenth century.　(*In the possession of Mrs Croly.*)

Croly, in which Salome and the head of John the Baptist are again represented, shows the same crowded design and finely wrought costume, and the same application of beads (Plate LXXXIII.).

The application of bugles, seed pearls, and spangles upon lace is a detail that cannot fail to strike the reader of the Wardrobe Accounts of Queen Elizabeth.*

The singular custom of representing religious subjects, both in lace, cutwork, and embroidery, became prominent towards the end of the reign of James I., and was a reflection of the Puritan taste.† "For flowers" now are made "Church histories."‡ Stuart raised embroideries, better known as stump work, have the costumes of the figures and various accessories covered with the stitch used in needlepoint lace.

Samplers carried on the tradition of cutwork, which was still made for "seaming" lace, for linen sheets,§ shirts, cupboard cloths, cushion cloths, &c., long after freer designs were in vogue for other uses. The latest sampler which includes a band of cutwork bears the date 1726.‖

A quantity of coarse lace continued apparently to be made in England until the eighteenth century, for the author of "Britannia Languens" complains that "the manufacture of linen was once the huswifery of English ladies, gentlewomen, and other women; now (1680) the huswifery women of England employ themselves in making an ill sort of lace, which serves no national or natural necessity."

A kind of work formed of very fine needlepoint stitches, with the pattern formed by a series of small pinholes, is the "hollie point," or

---

* In the New Year, 1559-60, the Countess of Worcester offers a ruff of lawn cutwork set with twenty small knobs like mullets, garnished with small sparks of rubies and pearls (Nichols, "Progresses of Queen Elizabeth").

† The linen of men and women was either so worked as to resemble lace, or was ornamented by the needle into representations of fruit and flowers, passages of history, &c. (Ben Jonson, "Every Man out of his Humour").

‡ "The City Match" (Jasper Mayne).

§ In Anne Hathaway's cottage in Shottery, Warwickshire, is shown the best linen sheet, which has a narrow strip about an inch and a half wide of cutwork joining the two breadths together, where there would otherwise be a seam. The pattern is of a simple zigzag character.

‖ In the possession of Mrs C. J. Longman.

holy point, which are so much used to ornament christening caps of
the seventeenth and eighteenth centuries. A sampler in the possession of Mrs Head * in most places has the linen completely cut away,
and the round or square holes so formed filled up with "hollie point,"
showing an initial or coronet, a small ornament like an acorn or a
fleur-de-lys, or a small diamond diaper pattern. Many of the small
designs are almost exactly reproduced in the crowns of some caps in
Mrs Head's collection. Some of the designs for hollie work are more
elaborate, and show a plant or an angular stem in a flower pot, or
two doves alighting on a flower.

* This sampler is dated 1728. It is illustrated in "The Sampler, its Development and Decay," by Mrs Head (*The Reliquary and Illustrated Archæologist*).

Plate LXXXIV.

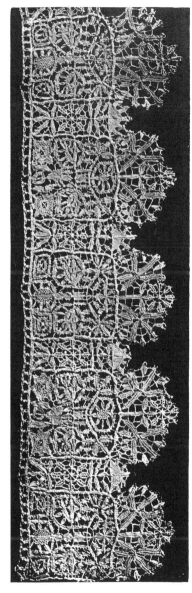

BORDERS OF NEEDLEPOINT.

English or Flemish, first half of seventeenth century.

Plate LXXXV.

ENGLISH NEEDLEPOINT SCALLOPS.
Early seventeenth century.

ENGLISH NEEDLEPOINT SCALLOPS.
Early seventeenth century. (*In the possession of Mr Sydney Vacher.*)

CHAPTER XVI.

ENGLISH BOBBIN LACE.

HONITON.

THE lace industry of Honiton is supposed to have been founded by Flemish refugees escaping from the Alva persecutions (1568-77), and names of undoubted Flemish origin occur at Honiton, at Colyton, and at Ottery St Mary. An early reference to lace-making is to be found in 1577 in Hellowes' "Familiar Epistles of Sir Anthonie of Gueuara," where he writes of seeing a woman "take her cushin for bone-lace or her rocke to spinne."* Shortly before 1620 a complaint was made by the London tradesmen of the influx of refugee artisans "who keep their misteries to themselves, which hath made them bould of late to device engines for workinge lace, and such wherein one man doth more than seven Englishmen can doe," which would seem to point not only to the national jealousy of the industrious immigrant but to the introduction of bobbin lace, which is more rapidly worked than needlepoint. The Honiton bone-lace manufacture, however, is already mentioned in 1620 by Westcote, and the often quoted inscription upon the tombstone of James Rodge, "Bone-lace siller" (d. 1617), in Honiton churchyard proves that the industry was well established in James I.'s reign.

Such lace as was made must have been similar to the insertions and vandyked edgings of twisted and plaited thread which had their origin in Italy. Though there are no authenticated specimens of bone-lace, "some early seventeenth-century sculptured monuments

* "The Familiar Epistles of Sir Anthonie of Gueuara, tr. out of the Spanish tongue by E. Hellowes," 1577.

bear well-preserved indications of geometric lace, as upon the monument to Lady Pole in Colyton Church (1623), and upon another to Lady Doddridge (1614) in Exeter Cathedral," which may represent the local manufacture.* The patterns of these have been copied by Mrs Treadwin, and specimens are shown in the Exeter Museum, titled " patent vandyke point."

Pins were imported from France till about 1626,† when the manufacture was introduced into England, and facilitated the making of lace. In 1636 the Countess of Leicester writes that " these bone-laces, if they be good are dear," and in the following year that they are " extremely dear."

From a petition sent to the House of Commons in 1698, when it was proposed to repeal the last preceding prohibition of foreign lace, we learn that " the English are now arrived to make as good lace in fineness and all other respects as any that is wrought in Flanders." Devonshire lace, indeed, must have followed much the same development as did Flemish. It was, however, on a much smaller scale, and far less was exported. The Flemish " send it to Holland, Germany, Sweden, Denmark, France, Spain, Portugal, &c., whereas we make it chiefly to serve our own country and plantations."

In the Diary of Celia Fiennes, who travelled through England in the time of William and Mary,‡ Honiton is again compared with Flemish laces. At Honiton, " they make the fine bone-lace in imitation of the Antwerp and Flanders lace, and indeed I think it as fine; it only will not wash so fine, which must be the fault in ye thread."

---

* A. S. Cole, *Journal of the Society of Arts*, 1st April 1904.

† In 1483 the importation of pins into England was prohibited by statute. In 1540 Queen Catherine received hers from France, and again in 1543 an Act was passed providing that " no person shall put to sale any pinnes but only such as shall be double-headed, and have the heads soldered fast to the shank of the pinnes, well smoothed, the shank well shapen, the points well and round filed, canted, and sharpened." To a large extent the supply of pins was received from France till about 1626, in which year the manufacture was introduced into Gloucestershire by John Tilsby. His business flourished so that he soon gave employment to 1,500 persons. In 1636 the pinmakers of London formed a corporation, and the manufacture was subsequently established at Bristol and Birmingham.

‡ " Through England on a Side Saddle in Time of William and Mary : The Diary of Celia Fiennes."

Plate LXXXVI.

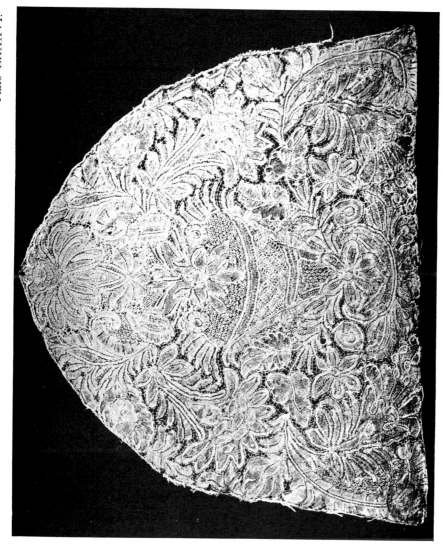

CAP CROWN.

Early Honiton (?), late seventeenth or eighteenth century.

Plate LXXXVII.

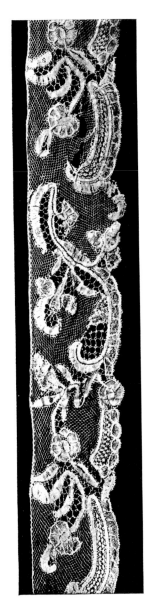
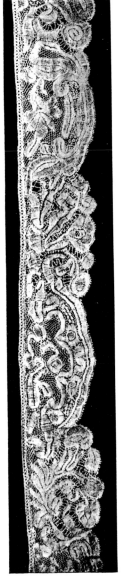

EDGINGS OF EARLY HONITON (?).

Early eighteenth century.

In the late eighteenth century, in an old diary, the lace trimming the wedding gown of Lady Harriet Strangways (1799) is described as "Brussels Honiton."

In the early eighteenth century lace-making claimed, when resenting a proposed tax, to be the second trade of the kingdom, but its importance was much exaggerated. It was, however, widely spread, and largely practised as a bye-industry. Later, in 1813, Vancouver writes of Devonshire that "its chief manufactures are the different kinds of woollen cloths, as also of bone-lace."

The English lace industry has always been hampered by the inferior quality of native flax,* which could not compete with that of Flanders. An attempt in the reign of Charles II. to induce Flemish lace-makers to settle in England was unsuccessful, and the manufacturing of linen was in a very rudimentary state on his accession.†

It is worth mentioning in this connection that Devon was formerly famous for its spinning. "As fine as Kerton (Crediton) spinning" is a proverb in the county. ‡

Early Devonshire lace is said to have had one peculiarity distinguishing it both from Brussels and from the later Honiton. This is the use of an outlining cordonnet, formed by massing together the

---

* The Maidstone authorities in the early seventeenth century complained that the thread-makers' trade was very much decayed by the importation of thread from Flanders ("List of Foreign Protestants resident in England, 1618-88," Camden Society).

"A body of Flemings who settled at Maidstone in 1567 carried on the thread manufacture ; flax spun for the threadmen being still known there as Dutch work" (Smiles, "The Huguenots in England and Ireland," 1868).

† "Perhaps," writes Strutt, "it was thought to be more greatly beneficial to procure the article (linen) by exchange than to make it at home, especially when the cultivation of hemp and flax was not conceived to be worth the attention of our farmers." In the fifteenth year of Charles II.'s reign an act was passed for the encouragement of the manufactures of all kinds of linen cloth and tapestry made from hemp or flax, by the virtue of which every person either a native or a foreigner might establish such manufactures in any place in England or Wales, without paying any acknowledgment, fee, or gratuity for the same.

‡ It is on record that one hundred and forty threads of woollen yarn spun in that town were drawn through the eye of a tailor's needle which was long exhibited there.

bobbins, just as is done nowadays to obtain slight veins of relief called brodes in Brussels appliqué.* But a piece of lace of the seventeenth or eighteenth century which can be assigned with certainty to Devonshire has yet to be found.

Three specimens in the Victoria and Albert Museum are tentatively attributed to old Honiton. The first two† are of rough workmanship and design (Plate LXXXVII.). In the third‡ (Plate LXXXVI.) the close plaiting of the flowers and other ornament is thrown into relief by occasional narrow margins, across which are threads linking the various portions together. These thread links are rather irregular, and group themselves into no series of definite meshes. This has been considered an eighteenth-century specimen of Devonshire pillow lace. It should be compared with a cap crown from the Musée des Arts Décoratifs, Brussels, attributed to Honiton. A "cloudiness" in the Victoria and Albert example, and a slightly coarser thread, suggests that it is English work.

A broad flounce of lace, belonging to Mrs Trew, in the style of Flemish lace towards the end of the seventeenth century, is attributed to Honiton, as "some forms in the lower border are characteristic of Honiton work. There is (it is said) also a marked absence of plan in the arrangement of details as well as in their treatment." This attribution appears doubtful.§

When the réseau ground was in vogue, Honiton was made first on the pillow by itself, and the réseau was then worked in round it, also on the pillow. "The plain pillow ground was very beautiful and regular, but very expensive. It was made of the finest thread procured from Antwerp, the market price of which in 1790 was £70 per pound."

---

* "Les guipures que vers la même époque (*i.e.*, early eighteenth century) on faisait en Angleterre, étaient du même genre, sauf que les différentes parties de l'ouvrage étaient reliées ensemble par des brides picotées et que, en outre, certaines portions du dessin étaient rehaussées de reliefs produits par une sorte de cordonnet que l'on obtenait en massant tous les fuseaux—comme nervures à relief appelées brodes dans l'application de Bruxelles,—on les rattachait ensuite par un crochetage" (Mme. Laurence de Laprade, "Le Poinct de France").

† Nos. 874, 1853 ; 864, 1853.

‡ No. 1368, 1855.

§ Catalogue of the *Daily Mail* Exhibition of British Lace, March 1908.

Plate LXXXVIII.

HONITON.

Late eighteenth or early nineteenth century. (*In the possession of Mrs Malkin.*)

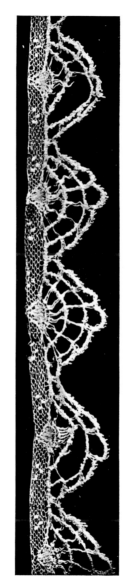

EDGING OF TROLLY LACE.

Thirteen-hole trolly, made near Exmouth, Devonshire.

.

With the introduction of machine-made net in the early part of the nineteenth century, the principle of appliqué work was also adopted in England, and the cheaper and inferior material was substituted for the hand-made ground. It is said that Queen Charlotte introduced the appliqué on net to encourage the new machine net.*

Honiton appliqué was most commonly of white thread sprigs mounted on thread net, but black silk sprigs were also made. These were made on the pillow with black silk, and were transferred to a fine machine-made silk net. No black laces have been made in Honiton for the last quarter of a century; they went out of fashion on account of the expense of the silk, which cost just double the price of linen thread.

The design of Honiton was derived from Flanders, partly no doubt because there was frequent intercommunication between the two countries. From 1700 downwards, though the edicts prohibiting the entry of Flanders lace were repealed, the points of France and Venice were still contraband.

The invention of machinery for lace-making was the greatest blow administered to the hand-made fabric. Heathcoat,† after his machinery at Loughborough had been destroyed by the Luddites, in 1811, established a factory at Tiverton for *bobbin* lace (so called because made of coarse thread by means of long bobbins), greatly to the injury of the bobbin-made lace for the next twenty years. The lace-makers have employed 2,400 hands in the town and neighbourhood, writes Lysons, but now (1822) not above 300 are employed.

"From about 1820 the Honiton workers introduced a most hideous set of patterns, designed," they said, "out of their own heads. 'Turkey tails,' 'frying pans,' 'bullocks' hearts,' and the most senseless sprigs and borderings took the place of the graceful compositions of the old school."‡ Mrs Bury Palliser tried to provide some families

* It took because it was so much cheaper. Designs upon old pillow net cost more than four times those upon the machine net.

† In 1809 Heathcoat took a patent for his bobbin-net machine.

‡ With regard to the design of Honiton M. Charles Blanc writes: "Un principe de goût à observer dans le dessin des dentelles, c'est de n'y pas mettre des objets trop nettement définis, tels qu'un vase, une corbeille, une couronne, un cœur de bœuf, une queue de dindon. Plus ces objets sont fidèlement imités, plus ils sont malséants dans le dentelle" ("L'Art dans la Parure et le Vêtement").

with new patterns of roses and leaves instead of the old "Duchess of Kents," "Brunswicks," and "Snowballs," but with little success. To this succeeded a period of floral patterns, directly copied from nature, which may be studied in the sprigs preserved at the Exeter Museum made for the Paris Exhibition of 1867. Later, the design again relapsed.

In a Parliamentary Report upon the lace industry of England, Mr Alan Cole writes of Honiton (1888): "A lace-worker at Beer says, 'Sometimes we see a new wall-paper and prick a pattern off it, changing a bit here, or leave a little, or add a little.' Another adapted her patterns from wall-paper, table-cloths, or *anything*." The sprigs thus derived out of cottage wall-papers were made separately, and sold to some other worker to join together in one confused patchwork. If patterns of a different character were chosen the workers declared "the gentlefolks called it machine."

About 1845 the application of Honiton sprigs was superseded by "guipure," *i.e.*, the sprigs, when made, were united on the pillow, or else joined by the needle, like the kindred "Duchesse" of Belgium. As a class, the details in foreign guipures are far better drawn, shaped, and arranged together than the English, and the execution is more finished and delicate.

Gimp* is the coarse glazed thread which is sometimes seen inside the edges of leaves and flowers. It gives stability to the lace, and is often used as a substitute for the raised work, being much more quickly made. The close portions of the toilé are worked in close stitch, or whole stitch.

The open lighter parts of the sprays are worked in lace-stitch or half stitch, the principle of which is that only one bobbin works across the leaf each time. You treat the bobbins in pairs, but the working pair is constantly changing; therefore one thread runs straight across, and the others slant down the work crosswise.

The raised work is the distinguishing mark of Honiton. In no other English lace is it introduced, and the value of a piece is estimated

---

* "Gimp is the shiny and coarse glazed thread used in Honiton and other pillow laces to mark out and slightly raise certain edges of the design, as a substitute for raised work" ("Caulfield and Saward's Dictionary," 1882).

Plate LXXXIX.

SPECIMENS OF HONITON.
First half of nineteenth century.
(In the Exeter Museum.)

"VANDYKE POINT."
In imitation of early geometrical lace.
(Given by Mrs Treadwin to the Exeter Museum.)

according to the raised work in it. The fillings of the flowers are done with plaitings which are largely used in Maltese and other laces.

The Honiton pillows run rather smaller than the Buckinghamshire ones, and do not have the numberless starched coverings—only three pill cloths over the top, and another each side of the lace in progress; two pieces of horn called sliders go between to take the weight of the bobbins from dragging the stitches in progress; a small square pin-cushion is on one side, and stuck into the pillow, the "needlepin," a large sewing needle in a wooden handle used for picking up loops. The bobbins are of neatly turned boxwood, small and light.*

The trade of lace-making remained for several generations in some families; thus (in 1871) an old lace-maker was discovered at Honiton, whose "turn," or wheel for winding cotton, had the date 1678 rudely carved on its foot.

DEVONSHIRE TROLLY.

Devonshire trolly, which has no affinity with Honiton, is very like the laces made in the Midlands, but of coarser thread, and not so well made. Lappets and scarves were made of trolly lace in the eighteenth century, and a trolly "head" is mentioned in 1756. "It was made," writes Mrs Palliser, "of coarse British thread with heavier and larger bobbins, worked straight on round and round the pillow. The name is said to be derived from the Flemish "trolle kant." It is quite extinct. An informant, writing from East Budleigh in 1896, says: "Some of the very old women here make beautiful trolly lace, but no young person. This is partly owing to there being no prickings left, for one of the old workers told me that when the lace trade was bad they used up their prickings as stiffenings for their waist belts, thinking they should never need them again." The

* "The bobbins used in Devonshire are always made of wood, and are perfectly plain and smooth in outline, and very light of weight. The custom of ornamenting bobbins does not appear to have been general in the West of England, and when any decoration is found, it is confined to simple incised patterns, coloured red, blue, or black, or a curious tortoise-shell mottling" ("A Note on Lace-Bobbins," Mrs Head, *The Connoisseur*, vol. x.).

specimens described as Devonshire trolly in the Exeter Museum cannot be distinguished from the Midland.* The specimen illustrated in Plate LXXXVIII. was bought in Somerset, and was recognised by a woman at Exmouth as "thirteen-hole trolly," such as was made about Exmouth, the last maker dying only a few years ago. Heavy bobbins compared with Honiton, were used, and no gingles. Some old trolly prickings leave the net unpricked as in one class of Valenciennes lace.

* 19th August 1708. "Last Thursday Mrs Bedingfield was married in white damask with silver troley on the petticoat" ("MSS. of the Earl of Dartmouth," Hist. MSS. Comm., vol. iii.).

Plate XC.

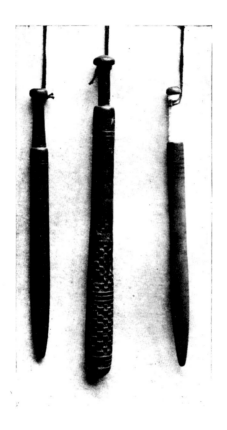

BEER, BRANSCOMBE, AND TROLLY BOBBINS.

CHAPTER XVII.

ENGLISH BOBBIN LACES.

MIDLAND AND OTHER ENGLISH LACES.

LACE-MAKING was formerly practised to a small extent in Hertford-shire, Derbyshire, Oxfordshire, Somerset, and Hampshire, besides in the better-known centres of Devonshire, Buckinghamshire, Bedford-shire, and Northamptonshire. Lace was made in Wales at Swansea, Pontardawe, Llanwrtyd, Dufynock, and Brecon, but never of any beauty.* It was formerly made at Ripon in Yorkshire, and in 1862 one old woman still continued working at a narrow edging with a small lozenge-shaped pattern known in local parlance by the name of "four-penny spot." This lozenge torchon-like pattern is the simplest type of lace, and was also made in Scotland, where it was known as "Hamilton" from its patroness, the Duchess of Hamilton, who introduced the manufacture at Hamilton in 1752. The edgings made there "were of a coarse thread, always of the lozenge pattern." Being strong and firm, it was used for night-caps, never for dresses, and justified the description of a lady who described it as of little account and spoke of it as "only Hamilton." The three specimens illustrated may be of this or of the similar Ripon manufacture (Plate XCI.).

The lace industry in Bedfordshire and Buckinghamshire has been attributed to Flemish immigrants, who fled from Alva's persecutions. A good quality of lace—to judge from its price—was made in

---

* Mrs Palliser, "History of Lace."

Buckinghamshire * in 1678, the highest prices ranging above thirty shillings a yard, while in Dorset and Devon—more important centres— six pounds per yard was occasionally reached. In the eighteenth century Buckinghamshire lace is declared to be " not much inferior to those from Flanders," † and occupied an important place in the trade of the counties.‡ But the only influence to be detected in Buckinghamshire laces is that of Lille, which is closely copied,§ probably after the advent of the settlers from the French provinces bordering on Flanders after the Revocation of the Edict of Nantes. There was a later influx of " ingenious French emigrants " at the time of the French Revolution, which was expected to improve the native manufacture. ‖

The chief centres in the lace industry in Buckinghamshire were at Great Marlow, Olney, Stony Stratford, Newport Pagnell,¶ and High Wycombe. There the lace was collected from the workers, for the industry itself was very widely spread in most of the villages in the county. In Bedfordshire, both Bedford and Woburn were important centres in the eighteenth century, and as late as 1863 the lace schools of Bedfordshire were more considerable than those in Devonshire.

" The duties of a lace schoolmistress were to insist on a certain amount of work being done, and if moral suasion was not sufficient, a cane was ready for use. The other duties of the mistress were to

---

* In 1623, the bone-lace trade was already " much decayed " in Buckinghamshire (State Papers, Dom. Jac. I., vol. 142, P.R.O.).

† " Magna Britannia."

‡ 1st October 1786.—The Marquis of Buckingham to W. W. Grenville : " Your doubts upon the thread lace have alarmed me extremely. . . . When I look to the numbers employed and to the effects which a revolution in that trade may bring upon the property of this country. For God's sake ! let me hear from you as soon as you can upon it ; but remember how deeply I am pledged to our manufactory by the importance of it to our own land " (" MSS. of J. B. Fortescue, Esq.," Hist. MSS. Comm., Thirteenth Report, appendix, part iii.).

§ Hence Bucks laces have been called " English Lille." Lille was very popular in England. One-third of the lace manufactured in the Dép. du Nord was smuggled into England in 1789.

‖ Annual Register, 1794.

¶ " This town is a sort of staple for bone-lace, of which more is thought to be made here than any town in England " (Lysons, " Magna Britannia ").

Plate XCI.

INSERTIONS AND EDGING OF ENGLISH BOBBIN LACE.
About beginning of nineteenth century.

Plate XCII.

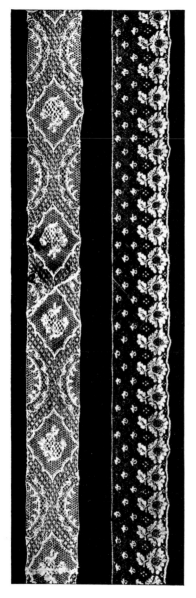

INSERTION AND EDGING OF BUCKINGHAMSHIRE LACE.

Late eighteenth century.

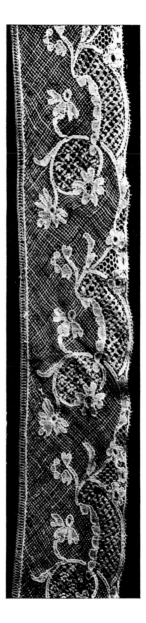

EDGING OF BUCKINGHAMSHIRE LACE.

prick the parchment (on which the pattern had been previously designed), also to buy the material for the work, to wind the bobbins by means of a small wheel and strap, and finally, to sell the lace to the lace-buyer, deducting a small sum for the house-room, firing, candles, &c."*

Fuller in his "Worthies" (1662) notes that in respect of manufactures, Northamptonshire "can boast of none worth the naming"; and in the eighteenth century its lace is not mentioned so frequently as that of Bedfordshire and Bucks. Anderson mentions that Kettering had "a considerable trade in lace," and fine lace was made at Middleton Cheney; Spratton, Paulerspury, and Towcester † were also centres of the trade. At the beginning of the nineteenth century, Wellingborough and the villages on the south-west side of the county appear to have had the largest number of lace-workers.

In connection with the lace industry, it is of interest to note that pin-making was also carried on in the county.

While the laces of Buckinghamshire, Bedfordshire, and Northamptonshire may be classed together, there are certain differences in the productions of each county—differences in quality rather than type. The finest and widest lace was, without doubt, made in North Buckinghamshire; it is made in narrow strips, afterwards invisibly joined; in that district the bobbins are small, and have very ornamental gingles. In South Buckinghamshire, Northamptonshire, and in Oxfordshire the bobbins are larger, the work not so refined. In Bedfordshire there is more gimp and less cloth (toilé) used, and in Buckinghamshire more cloth and less gimp.

In 1778, according to M'Culloch, ‡ was introduced the "point ground," as it is locally termed—the réseau ground, like that of Lille, composed of two threads twisted, and simply crossed not plaited, at their junction. "The mesh varies a little in shape from a four-sided

---

* "Victoria History of the County of Northampton," vol. ii.

† "This place is remarkable for a manufactory of lace and silk stockings which employs most of the meaner inhabitants" ("A Northern Tour from St Albans," 1768, MSS. of the Earl of Verulam, Hist. MSS. Comm.).

‡ "Dict. of Commerce."

diamond to a hexagon, according as the threads at crossing are drawn tighter or left loose and long." *

The untwisted outline thread is called locally the trolly. In design the oval-shaped openings filled with light, open modes are closely copied from Lille, as are also the square dots; arranged in groups of three and four—the " points d'esprit" of Lille—which are to be found especially in the narrow " baby " laces.

In some specimens of trolly lace in the Victoria and Albert Museum the design resembles that of some Mechlin laces made early in the eighteenth century. The réseau is composed of six-pointed star-meshes, which was often made in Buckinghamshire. Another piece of trolly has four varieties of fillings-in, which almost suggest that it is part of a sampler lace exhibited by lace-makers to encourage their patrons to select groundings to their particular taste.

The ground sometimes known as " wire ground," " cat stitch," and " French ground," was introduced about the time of the Regency, and although in many cases effective, has to be most skilfully arranged and interwoven with the pattern, otherwise a heavy-looking lace is the result.

During the Regency a point lace, as it was called, with the toilé on the edge, was for many years in fashion, and was named Regency point. It is illustrated in Fig. 145 in Mrs Palliser's "History of Lace," edition 1902.

After the Exhibition of 1851 were introduced Maltese guipures or plaited laces, a variety grafted on to the Maltese type. The ground is composed of a trellis of the characteristic Maltese oval enlargement, and the pattern is like that of the Buckinghamshire lace, but heavier. A very coarse cordonnet is used (Plate XCIV.).

Run laces were laces in which the pattern, light and generally floral, was run in with the needle upon a pillow-made ground.

" On the breaking out of the war with France, the closing of our ports to French goods gave an impetus to trade, and the manufacturers undertook to supply the English market with lace similar to that of Normandy"; hence a sort of English Valenciennes. In the specimen illustrated this net is probably made as for trolly lace, without pins, and a gimp is given instead of the Valenciennes edge.

* A. M. S., " Point and Pillow Lace."

Plate XCIII.

EDGING OF "ENGLISH MECHLIN."
Made in North Buckinghamshire.

EDGING OF "ISLE OF WIGHT" LACE.
Run lace.

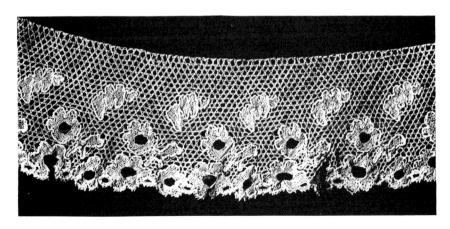

EDGING OF BUCKINGHAMSHIRE LACE.
Coarse quality.

Plate XCIV.

SPECIMENS OF BEDFORD MALTESE.
Called " Plaited Lace" (*cir.* 1851).

EDGING OF BUCKINGHAMSHIRE LACE.

EDGING OF NORTHAMPTONSHIRE LACE.

"English Mechlin" was made in North Bucks. The design is an exact copy of late Mechlin, where the pattern consists of a series of stiff sprigs or flowers with small leaflets, and perhaps a further ornamentation of spots upon the ground near the pattern. The net in the English Mechlin differs from the Mechlin réseau, and is not so regular (Plate XCIII.).

In Buckinghamshire lace "the shape of the pillow varies in the different parts of the county, in the North Bucks workers use a round, hardly stuffed straw cushion, while in Central and Mid Bucks the pillow used is longer and thinner.*

The larger bobbins are called gimps; these hold the coarser or silky-looking linen thread which marks the outline and accentuates the pattern, and which is one of the characteristics of Buckinghamshire lace. The "tallies" are four bobbins used to make the small square dots; these have metal bands twisted round them, to distinguish them from the ordinary lace bobbins.

The number of bobbins necessary varies according to the width of the lace, a narrow edging requiring from two to three dozen, and a wider one several hundred; even so many as a thousand are required for a very wide pattern, but in this case it is necessary to have an extremely large pillow, otherwise the bobbins would fall over the sides and become entangled.

A special kind of oak chest is a relic of the prosperous days of lace-making in Buckinghamshire.† The upper part was intended to hold the lace pillow, while the two shallow drawers below were for the bobbins and patterns.

Of the Wiltshire lace manufacturers in the past we know little. Lady Arundel in the seventeenth century alludes incidentally to the "bone lace" of North Wiltshire,‡ and there were lace schools in the

---

* M. E. Burrowes, "Buckinghamshire Lace," *Art Workers' Quarterly*, January 1904.

† One of these chests, dated 1702, is illustrated in "Point and Pillow Lace," by A. M. S., p. 178.

‡ Describing the destruction of the leaden pipes at Wardour by the soldiers she says, "They cut up the pipe and sold it, as these men's wives in North Wiltshire do bone lace, at sixpence a yard."

county at the time of the Great Plague.* A little later, Aubrey, the
Wiltshire historian and antiquary, complains that the "shepherdesses
of Salisbury Plain" of late years (1680) do begin to work point
whereas before they did only knitt coarse stockings." Malmesbury
was one of the Wiltshire centres, and also Downton near Salisbury.
The better Downton lace is very like the narrow and coarser Buckinghamshire,† and the ground is like that of Buckinghamshire, only
worked without a pin in each mesh. The net is worked down from
the head to the foot, and only pinned at the foot and the head. The
workers call the net "bar-work." Other patterns are exactly like
those illustrated as characteristic of Suffolk. The "French ground"
is also used, which is the same as the Buckinghamshire "cat-stitch"
or "French ground," and is made with pins.

In Dorset the lace manufacture was already extinct about the
early years of the nineteenth century, and no trace is left of its
character, though Lyme Regis, Blandford, and Sherborne all made
expensive laces of good quality. A few workers remained in Char-
mouth in 1891. Blandford in especial, according to Defoe, made
"the finest bone lace in England . . . and which, they said, they
rated above £30 a yard."

Some bobbin lace used to be made in the Isle of Wight, but what
is known as "Isle of Wight" lace was made on machine net, the
pattern outlined with a run thread, filled in with needlepoint stitches.
The late Mechlin designs were chiefly copied. In 1900 there were
only two or three old women workers left.

Suffolk has produced bobbin lace of little merit. The make of
lace resembles that of Buckinghamshire and Downton lace, and that
of Norman laces of the present time. In a number of specimens in
the Victoria and Albert Museum the entire collection displays varied
combinations of six ways of twisting and plaiting threads. The
mesh is very large and open ; a coarse outlining thread is used to give
definition to the simple pattern (Plate XCV.).

At Coggeshall in Essex tambour lace was worked, and a specimen
in the Victoria and Albert Museum was made by a survivor late in
the nineteenth century. This town was the first, and is now the only,

---

* Waylem, "History of Marlborough."

† Many of the old patterns are the same as the Buckinghamshire ones.

Plate XCV.

SPECIMENS OF INSERTION AND NARROW EDGINGS.

Made in Suffolk.

place where tambour is produced in England. "The pattern is worked in chain-stitch upon a foundation of bobbin net by means of a fine crochet hook screwed into a bone handle. The net is first stretched evenly upon a frame. Originally this frame was round, like the head of a drum or tambourine—hence its name. Now, however, the frame is composed usually of two long parallel pieces of wood, with movable cross-bars. The thread, which is first wound by the worker upon a spool revolving on a spindle affixed to the frame, is passed through her left hand beneath the net, caught by a needle rapidly, and dexterously manipulated by the right hand above." Open work may be introduced. "So far as can be ascertained in the absence of any written record, the tambour lace industry was first introduced into England by a French *emigré*, Drago or Draygo, who, accompanied by his daughters, settled in Coggeshall in the nineteenth ceutury. The exact date is not known, but may be assumed to have been between 1810 and 1823." * In the latter year Heathcoat's patent for a bobbin-net machine, invented in 1809, expired, and lace frames were set up by hundreds, with the result that the price fell in a few years from £5 per square yard to 8d. or less. In Pigot's Directory of 1832, three names appear in Coggeshall as "lace manufacturers." About 1851† the industry was at its height, but after 1859 a decline was observable. After a revival in 1866 the industry sank again, until in 1901 there were but 222 workers.

* "The Victoria County History of Essex," vol. ii.

† Some fine specimens were shown at the Great Exhibition, but unfortunately under the head of Nottingham Lace.

104

CHAPTER XVIII.

IRISH LACES.

CARRICKMACROSS AND LIMERICK.

THE two characteristic Irish laces are more nearly allied to embroidery than to lace proper, and are of comparatively late introduction. Of these, the first, Carrickmacross, dating from the year 1820, consists of a pattern cut in cambric and applied to a net ground. The second, Limerick tambour lace, was first introduced in 1829 A class of English silk tambour * or chain-stitch embroidery with coloured silks or cotton, which was made during the later seventeenth and early eighteenth centuries, shows strong traces of Indian influence, but the application of chain-stitch to a net ground does not seem to have been known in England until about 1820.

Charles Walker, a native of Oxfordshire, who had married a "lady who was mistress of an extensive lace manufactory in Essex," established a fabric at Mount Kennet, Limerick, in 1829. The design and workmanship of the lace produced before his death in 1842, are much superior to those of later specimens. He brought with him to Ireland twenty-four young women skilled in the art of lace embroidery as teachers, of whom several came from Coggeshall.

* On a frame is stretched a piece of net. A floss thread or cotton is then drawn by a hooked or tambour needle through the meshes of the net. In run lace, finer and lighter than tambour, the pattern is formed with finer thread which is not drawn in with the tambour, but run in with the point needle.

Plate XCVI.

105

CHAPTER XIX.

BLONDES.

BLONDE * laces were first introduced in 1745 † and were known as nankins or blondes; their name of "blond" comes from their original Venetian name, "merletti biondi," pale laces. De Gheltof informs us that it was given by the authority of the magistrates of Mercanzia, in 1759. The first silk used for the new production was of its natural unbleached colour, afterwards a brilliant white silk took its place.

The blonde of the time of Louis XVI. was a very light fabric with spots, the ground is sometimes specified as " fond d'Alençon."

The "Livre-Journal de Madame Eloffe" notes blonde fond noisette, blonde à bouquets, blonde fond Alençon à poix. "There are but few details of close work (mat), the ornament being principally in outline wrought sinuously with a single thread, thereby producing a diversity of interlacing open forms,"‡ and this style was revived at Caen about 1840, when quantities of such work was produced. At various periods, but especially during the eighteenth century, blondes were produced with a cordonnet of chenille, or of gold thread, and sometimes the "mats" were of coloured silks;§ the patterns are

---

* Beck's " Draper's Dictionary."

    † " A vandyke in frize your neck must surround.
      Turn your lawns into gauze, let your Brussels be blond."
                      (*Universal Magazine*, 1754.)

  ‡ E. Lefébure, " Broderie et Dentelles."

  § " On y adjoignait, vers la fin du XVIIIe siècle des perles taillés dont les facettes recevaient et renvoyaient la lumière " (M. Charles et L. Pagès, " Les Broderies et les Dentelles ").

similar to Alençon of that date, floral or ornamented with detached bouquets or flowers, or with spots (poix). In 1787, it is noted that the taste for Alençon and Argentan has given way to a taste for blondes. According to the Duchesse d'Abrantès, they were a "summer" lace.* And it was during her later years that Marie Antoinette wore considerable quantities of the light patterned blonde laces.

The classical motifs of the Empire followed; a robe of Marie Louise with a heavy border of oval motifs, the ovals outlined with a fine silver thread, was exhibited at the Musée Galliera in 1904. Since the Empire,† and especially during the Second Empire, the floral and florid Spanish taste in blondes has prevailed; with big motifs worked in close work, standing out in contrast to the delicate ground.

Blondes were made at Chantilly, Caen, Bayeux,‡ and Le Puy, and there were besides several smaller manufactures which have disappeared leaving no trace.

At Chantilly, noted for its black silk lace, white blondes, which were fashionable in Paris in 1805, were much made until 1835, when black lace again came into vogue.

At Bayeux the fabric of silk blonde, which had died out, was revived in 1827, and "blondes mates" were made there with great success until 1870, when machine-made blondes replaced the hand-made lace.

At Le Puy, which suffered from over-production in the early eighteenth century, a manufacture of blondes and silk lace was introduced in 1761 to employ the people in a more lucrative way.‖ A report written in 1771 states that this fabric occupies all the inhabitants

---

* The Duchesse d'Abrantès, who married in the year 1800, describing her trousseau, mentions " garnitures de robes en blonde pour l'été."

† A manufacture of blonde at Bourg-Argental, which dated from 1758, applied in 1778 for aid to the Government. Manufactures were established at Nonancourt (near Dreux) in 1770, and at Orbic in 1793. Sassenage, in Dauphiné, petitioned for a grant for its manufacture of blondes in 1772.

‡ Blondes were very popular from 1825 to 1845 ; Caen, Bayeux, and Chantilly employed half their lace-workers at making it.

§ A report written in 1771 by De Fage, Commissaire Principal du Roi à l'Assiette du Puy. Quoted by Mme. Laurence de Laprade in " Le Poinct de France."

of Le Puy and the entire diocese. The silk came from the merchants of Lyons, who imported the white from Pekin and Nankin, the black from Provence and Valencia; but they mixed it with an inferior quality of silk from Nîmes. It was sold very cheaply, and was little esteemed owing to the inferior quality of silk introduced.

Anderson writes that up to 1780 much blonde, both black and white, and of various colours, was made at Sherborne in Dorset, of which a supply was sent to all markets. From the later years of the eighteenth century the lace trade of Sherborne declined and gradually died out. In 1773 the *Annual Register* mentions an institution under royal patronage for "usefully employing female infants, especially those of the poor, in the blond black silk lace, and thread lace manufactures at No. 14 Mary-la-bone Lane."

A manufacture imitating French blondes was set up in Venice towards the close of the eighteenth century, and about the same period, black blonde in imitation of Chantilly was made at Genoa.

Spanish blondes do not equal in workmanship those of Bayeux and Chantilly, either in the firmness of the ground or regularity of the pattern. Of specimens bearing date from 1810 to 1840, "some have much resemblance to the fabric of Lille—clear hexagonal ground, with the pattern worked in one coarse thread—others of a double ground, the designs flowers." Barcelona, near which is a silk-throwing manufactory, is the centre of the Spanish manufacture of blondes.

GLOSSARY OF TERMS.

APPLIQUÉ.—Lace where the ornament is made separately, and then fixed and sewn by hand to a ground of bobbin or machine made net.

ARGENTELLA.—*See* Réseau Rosacé, p. 68.

BARS.—*See* Brides.

BOBBIN LACE.—*See* Pillow Lace.

BOBBINS.—Small elongated wooden or bone reels on which the thread is wound for the purpose of pillow-lace making. They are frequently ornamented with patterns pricked or stained, and polished. They are weighted with "gingles" or "jingles," *i.e.*, beads, coins, seals, seeds, or various other small articles.

BONE LACE.—A term applied in England, during the sixteenth and seventeenth centuries, to bobbin-made lace.

BRIDES.—A small strip or connection, linking the details of ornament in lace. It may consist of (1) threads overcast with button-hole stitches, or (2) of twisted or plaited threads. The word is French, the English equivalent being pearl-tie. The French word is chiefly employed.

BRIDES PICOTÉES.—Brides ornamented with small picots, or minute loops.

BURATTO.—Darned net in which the twisted network was made by passing the foundation threads forwards and backwards in a frame. The name Buratto comes from the sieves made in this way in Italy for sifting grain and meal.*

BUTTON-HOLE STITCH.—The chief stitch in needle-made lace, also known as *point de boutonnière* (*not* point noué, as it is described in many books on lace).

* Mrs John Hungerford Pollen, "Seven Centuries of Lace," 1908.

CARTISANE.—A strip of parchment or vellum covered with silk or metal thread, used to form a pattern.

CHAMP.—*See* Fond.

CORDONNET.—The outline to ornamental forms. The cordonnet consists (1) of a single thread, or (2) of several threads worked together to give the appearance of one large thread, or (3) of a thread or horse-hair overcast with button-hole stitches.

COXCOMBS.—Old English term for bars (brides).

DENTÉLÉ.—Scalloped edge.

DROSCHEL.—Flemish word used for net ground made with bobbins.

ENGRÊLURE.—Footing or heading, to the *upper* end to a lace which is used to sew the lace on to the material it is to decorate.

ENTOILAGE.—*See* Fond.

FILET BRODÉ.—*See* Lacis, Chapter II.

FILLINGS.—A word occasionally used for *modes* or *jours;* fancy openwork stitches employed to fill in enclosed spaces in both needle-made and bobbin-made laces.

FOND.—Identical with *champ, entoilage,* and *treille.* The groundwork of needle-made or bobbin lace, as distinct from the toilé or pattern which it surrounds.

FOND CHANT.—*See* Chantilly chapter, p. 82.

FOND SIMPLE.—Sometimes called *fond de Lille.* The sides of the meshes are not partly plaited as in Brussels or Mechlin, nor wholly plaited as in Valenciennes; but four of the sides are formed by twisting two threads round each other, and the remaining two sides by simply crossing over each other.

FOOTING.—*See* Engrêlure.

GIMP.—The *pattern* which rests on the ground or is held together by brides. In Honiton and the Midlands, the word denotes the coarse glazed thread used like a cordonnet to emphasise the edges of the design.

GINGLES.—*See under* Bobbins.

GREEK LACE.—Trade name for cutwork, or reticella.

GRILLÉ.—The openwork on the toilé of bobbin lace, as contrasted with the *mat.*

GROPPO [Ital.].—A knot or tie.

GROUNDS.—The grounds of lace are divided into two classes, one being called the *bride*, the other the *réseau*. The *bride* ground is formed with plain or ornamental bars, in order to connect the ornaments forming the pattern. The *réseau* ground is a net made with the needle, or with bobbins, to connect the ornaments forming the pattern.

HEADING.—*See* Engrêlure.

HOLLIE POINT.—*See* English Needlepoint, p. 87.

JOURS.—*See* Fillings.

LACIS.—*See* Chapter Lacis.

LEGS.—Bars.

MACRAMÉ.—A hand-made knotted fringe. *See* Knotted Fringes, Chapter IV.

MAT.—The close-work of bobbin lace, as opposed to the grillé.

MERLETTI A PIOMBINI.—Bobbin lace (piombini = small leaden bobbins).

MERLETTO [Ital.].—Lace.

MEZZO PUNTO.—Lace in which the pattern is formed by braid or tape, and in which the brides and fillings are of needlepoint.

MODANO.—A general name in Italy for square-meshed laces.

MODES.—Jours, fillings.

PASSEMENT.—Until the seventeenth century lace in France was called passement, a word originally used of embroideries to lay flat over garments, to ornament them. The word passement continued to be used till the middle of the seventeenth century.

PEARL EDGE.—A narrow thread edge of projecting loops used to sew cn to lace as a finish to its edge.

PEARLS or PURLS.—Bars.

PICOT.—Minute loops worked on to the edge of a bride or cordonnet, or added as an enrichment to the ornament, as in rose point.

PILLOW LACE (or BOBBIN LACE).—Lace made on the pillow by twisting and plaiting threads. Fr. Dentelle au fuseau.

PIZZO [Ital.].—Lace.

PLY.—Single untwisted thread.

POINT COUPÉ.—French term for cutwork.

POINT DE NEIGE.—A name given to a fine quality of Italian rose point, with many small raised flowers, enriched with clusters of picots.

POINT DE PARIS.—The designation of the réseau also known as the fond chant. It has been claimed that a special kind of lace was known by this name. Manufacture of simple kind of lace was certainly carried on during the seventeenth and eighteenth centuries in the Ile de France and in Paris itself.

POINT DE RACCROC.—A stitch used by lace-makers to join réseau ground.

POINT LACE.—Lace made with the needle (point à l'aiguille). The term *point* has been misused to describe varieties of lace, such as point d'Angleterre, de Malines, de Milan, which are laces bobbin-made, and not made with the needle.

POINT PLAT.—A French term for needle-made lace, without any raised work.

POTTEN KANT.—*See* Antwerp Lace, p. 53.

PRICKED.—A term used in bobbin-lace making to denote the special marking out of the pattern upon parchment.

PRICKER.—An instrument used in bobbin-lace making to prick holes in the pattern to receive the pins.

PUNTO [Ital.]—A stitch.

PUNTO IN ARIA.—*Lit.* "stitch in air," used (1) of an embroidery stitch; (2) of all Italian needlepoint laces, made without any foundation of net or linen; thus strictly speaking including rose point, and point de Venese à réseau.

PUNTO TIRATO.—Drawn thread-work.

PURLINGS.—A stitch used in Honiton guipure to unite the bobbin-made sprigs.

PURLS.—Brides.

RÉSEAU.—A ground of small regular meshes (1) either made on the pillow in various manners, or (2) by the needle in less elaborate manners.

RÉSEAU ROSACÉ, OR ARGENTELLA.—*See* Chapter on Alençon and Argentan, p. 68.

RÉZEL or RESEUIL.—*See* Lacis, Chapter II., p. 7 *et seq.*

ROSE POINT.—Needlepoint lace with raised work upon it.

RUNNERS.—The name by which the bobbins which work across a pattern in bobbin lace are known.

SEMÉS.—Powderings of small ornamental details, such as spots, sprigs, &c., upon the ground.

TELA TAGLIATA.—Cut linen, edged by button-hole stitch and joined by brides.

TOILÉ.—The pattern or work of closer texture on both needlepoint and bobbin-made laces. Toilé is so called because it resembles toile or linen.

TRINA [Ital.].—Lace.

INDEX.

NOTE.—*References in Roman figures are to Plates.*

B